THE GLORY OF PREACHING

Clarence DeLoach and Jay Lockhart

The Jenkins Institute
www.thejenkinsinstitute.com

Published by The Jenkins Institute

www.thejenkinsinstitute.com

ISBN: 0615950442
ISBN-13: 978-0615950440 (The Jenkins Institute)

DEDICATION

To every faithful preacher of the Gospel who desires to be an expositor of the Word of God.

The Authors

CONTENTS

FOREWORD

In the preface to John Stott's classic work, *Between Two Worlds*, Michael Green writes, "Much of the current uncertainty about the gospel and the mission of the church must be due to a generation of preachers which have lost confidence in the Word of God."

In the intervening thirty years since that statement was made churches around the world have attempted everything imaginable to recapture that certainty of the gospel and the mission of the church. The answer to the dilemma faced by the church today is a return to Biblical preaching.

We can think of no men more imminently qualified to help us renew this commitment to Biblical preaching than Clarence DeLoach and Jay Lockhart. These two wonderful veteran preachers have more than 100 combined years of proclaiming the unsearchable riches of Jesus. Brother DeLoach and brother Lockhart have preached the truth of God's Word in love around the world. Many souls have been won and many churches have been strengthened by their preaching.

The book you hold in your hand will restore your faith in expository preaching. It will renew in you a desire to help the church recapture that certainly of the gospel and the mission of the church.

The first section of the book makes a strong case for the great need for expository preaching. We are reminded of the passion we need as well as the priority, purpose, and power of expository preaching.

In part two the authors give us the nuts and bolts of expository preaching. We are given a great a definition of expository preaching.

We also learn how to prepare and deliver expository sermons that will build up the body of Christ.

The final section of the book contains actual expository sermons that have been preached by the authors. These outstanding sermons by themselves would be worth much more than the price of this book. In these sermons we find all of the elements of expository preaching that are discussed throughout the book.

Every preacher of the Gospel who reads these words will be blessed. Our preaching will be richer for having read these words. In addition those who listen to the preaching of the Word will be blessed. Through the writing of this book these two brothers have once again challenged us, mentored us, and encouraged us as preachers of the Word of God.

It is an honor and a privilege to recommend to you this outstanding volume. I join a grateful brotherhood in expressing our deep appreciation for the preaching as well as the life of Clarence DeLoach and Jay Lockhart.

Jeff A. Jenkins
Flower Mound, TX

INTRODUCTION

CLARENCE DELOACH

Nearly two years ago, I asked my friend and fellow gospel preacher Jay Lockhart to join with me in the production of this volume on preaching. We had in mind a work that would be helpful and encouraging to young preachers who would follow. We felt that if we could pass on some of the things we have learned in our nearly twelve decades of preaching, such a book might be beneficial.

William Quale once wrote, "Preaching is not the art of making a sermon and delivering it. Preaching is the art of making a preacher and delivering that."

Preaching is both a burden and a blessing, a passion and a privilege. We have seen the type of preaching that we have known fall upon bad times. Many preachers want anecdotes and "feel good" stories rather than presentation of the Word of God as we heard it in our youth. We live in a time of sophisticated technology. The media entertains us with color graphics and pictures. In contrast, preaching appears to be outdated, bland, and boring. Sadly, some in the church do not believe that it has much influence in the modern world. But it is the conviction of the authors of this volume that God has not changed His mind regarding the place and priority of preaching.

God has richly blessed my life and work as a preacher, and I am eternally grateful. I am indebted to many brethren who believed in me and encouraged me. My mother, who lived to be almost one hundred, encouraged me from my youth. She said that from a child, I preached: to the chickens, cows and cousins when they would listen. My first sermon was preached at my home congregation in Dickson County,

Tennessee, when I was the age of fifteen. I am thankful for so many — family, friends, and brethren — who supported my efforts.

E. Claude Gardner and W.A. Bradfield steered me toward Freed-Hardeman College. Men like Batsell Barrett Baxter, Ira North, Carrol Ellis, and Willard Collins were mentors at David Lipscomb College. B.C. Goodpasture, editor of the Gospel Advocate, was a blessing in my life. So many brethren have touched and influenced my life that for lack of space I could not name them.

I have found unfailing support from my family. My wife of fifty-six years, Eddie, has worked with me faithfully and heartily. My children are supportive. I am grateful to my daughter, Rhonda Clark, for typing the manuscript and to Dr. Sue Berry, a long-time family friend and teacher, for her encouragement and her expertise in editing the manuscript.

It is my fervent prayer that this work will be encouraging and helpful, especially to our young preachers who are being trained for ministry.

An old preacher once said, "To be listened to is the first thing; therefore, be interesting. To be understood is the second thing; therefore, be clear. To be useful is the third thing; therefore, be practical. To be obeyed is the fourth thing; therefore, speak as the oracles of God."

To these ends, this volume is prayerfully sent forth. To God be the glory!

Clarence DeLoach

INTRODUCTION

JAY LOCKHART

It was John Donne, a 17th century English Poet, who wrote in his *Meditation XVII* from *Devotions*: "No man is an island, entire of himself . . . ." Each one of us is a part of all those who have touched our lives. I am indebted to so many people: my parents, who trained me as a child and encouraged me to preach the gospel; my brother, Jim, who was always my hero; Ross Swindler and Paul Hall, my preachers at the Southside Church of Christ (Camden Avenue) in Parkersburg, West Virginia, who gave me my first opportunities to preach; my teachers at Freed Hardeman College (University), men like H. A. Dixon, W. Claude Hall, Frank Van Dyke, G. K. Wallace, E. Claude Gardner, and Thomas Scott, who shaped my early training in ministry; my mentors and teachers at David Lipscomb (University), including Batsell Barrett Baxter, Carl McKelvey, and Sue Berry, who refined my skills; older preachers, too numerous to mention by name, who helped in my development; younger preachers, who give me hope for the future of the church; contemporary preachers who are my friends; my children, Terry Shaw, Tammy Sanford, and Jay Paul Lockhart, Jr., who were always proud that their daddy was a preacher; each of the congregations with which I have worked as "local preacher"; and last, but by no means the least, my wife, Arlene, who has been my greatest encourager and sometimes my severest critic and who for all these years has worked quietly and diligently behind the scenes as the one I consider an ideal preacher's wife. To all of these and others, I want to say, "Thank you for blessing my life."

Also, I want to thank Dianne Little, the secretary for the Whitehouse Church, for typing the manuscripts, Arlene Lockhart for proofing these lessons, and Sue Berry, the finest college English teacher I ever knew, for correcting the finished copy. Finally, I thank my great friend, an outstanding preacher and writer in his own right, and a fine preacher of the gospel, Clarence DeLoach, for giving me the opportunity to co-author this book with him.

Jay Lockhart

PART 1

THE GLORY OF PREACHING

1

THE PASSION OF PREACHING

JAY LOCKHART

A BURNING FIRE IN MY BONES

From a human point of view Jeremiah was one of the most unsuccessful preachers of history. For forty years he spoke the message of God to a rebellious people, not many of whom wanted to hear the message. He was laughed at, ridiculed, beaten, put in stocks, imprisoned, thrown into a partially dry cistern, and threatened with death. He became so discouraged that he decided to quit. He said, "I will not make mention of Him, nor speak any more in His name" (Jer. 20:9—all Scripture quotations in this chapter will be from the NKJV unless otherwise noted). However, Jeremiah could not refrain from speaking for God, and he cried, "But His word was in my heart like a burning fire shut up in my bones; I was weary of holding it back, and I could not" (Jer. 20:9). Every preacher of the word must, like Jeremiah, speak because he has a fire burning in his bones. One trainer of preachers advised his preacher students, "Boys, don't preach unless you have to." There is something wonderfully worthwhile in this advice: those who preach must preach because they have to.

Several years ago an acquaintance called to say he was looking for a job. He had preached full time but was currently teaching on the college level. He said of his job search, "I'm not too good to try preaching again." He was advised to seek other employment as those who preach because they are "not too good to try preaching again" do a disservice to God, to themselves, and to the people with whom they work. There must be a fire in the bones of those who preach the word of God.

A PERSONAL JOURNEY

I cannot remember when I did not want to be a preacher. My mother told me that when I was a small child I would stand on a footstool with my Bible in hand and "preach." The only words that could be understood were "God" and "Jesus." When I was about five years old, my grandmother took care of a female cousin, about my age, and me while our mothers worked outside our homes. My cousin and I would "play church." We sang songs, prayed, took the communion of crackers and water, and I preached. My cousin enjoyed it all until it came time for "baptisms." I would throw her down on a throw rug, which was our "baptistry." She never did like that part of it.

The preaching fire grew in me during the following years. By the age of twelve I was earnest about being a preacher. When I attempted my first talk in a men's training class, I said about two sentences and sat down with tears in my eyes. The next week I tried again with the same results. Our preacher, Ross Swindler, insisted I get up again at the end of our class and read a passage of Scripture. He seemed to think that if I had failed in my first two attempts to speak before an audience, I might never get up again. That act of kindness and concern probably saved the day for me. Ross Swindler baptized me when I was twelve years old and encouraged me in every way to preach. I will ever be indebted to him for his wisdom in dealing with me as a twelve "year" old. When I was about sixteen, Paul Hall preached for my hometown congregation, the Southside church in Parkersburg, West Virginia. Paul invited several young men in the congregation to present short sermons before he preached on Sunday evenings, and at that time I began to prepare and deliver sermons. When I was eighteen, the elders of the church in Belpre, Ohio, just across the Ohio River from Parkersburg, asked me to preach on a Sunday evening. In this congregation, where my maternal grandparents worshipped, I presented my first "real sermon." I had it memorized, and I timed it to exactly thirty minutes. Eight minutes into that sermon I was half through, and the whole sermon lasted only twenty minutes; but I now had "a fire in my bones."

My preparation — my efforts to "stoke the fire" — led me to places and people who have enriched my life. Following high school I entered

Freed-Hardeman College, where I majored in Bible. During those three years I was tutored by some of the greatest men I have known. H.A. Dixon, the President of the school, taught me the dignity that should characterize a preacher. W. Claude Hall taught me how to laugh at myself and how to use proper English in preaching. Frank Van Dyke taught me logic. G.K. Wallace taught me how to put the Scriptures together in an orderly presentation. Thomas Scott taught me how to study. E. Claude Gardner gave my wife a job as his secretary, and her salary helped me stay in school. Brother Gardner also recommended me for a summer preaching appointment with a well-established congregation that gave me invaluable experience in the day-to-day work of the preacher. The fire continued to burn. After Freed-Hardeman I went to David Lipscomb, where I experienced one of the greatest blessings of my life. I sat at the feet of Batsell Barrett Baxter, who became my mentor in preaching. After graduating from Lipscomb, I began preaching full time and finished a Masters program at Harding Graduate School, where I had the privilege of studying with great men like W.B. West, Paul Rotenberry, and Jack Lewis. Finally, I finished a Ph.D. at Trinity Theological Seminary, where I was able to hone my skills for more effective church work. Through all these years the fire has burned brightly. During the course of more than fifty years I have preached for some fine churches as a local evangelist, including twenty-three years with the West Erwin church in Tyler, Texas. I have preached in meetings and lectureships for some of our outstanding congregations and have associated with some of the greatest people in the world – members of Jesus' church. These experiences have contributed to the "fire in my bones." I love to preach, and I always anticipate the next sermon. In my younger days I struggled with what I would preach next, but now I struggle with how I can preach all that I have planned. There's this "fire in my bones." An effective preacher will need this fire, this passion.

CULTIVATING PASSION

If one must have fire in his bones to be an effective preacher, how does he acquire this passion? *First*, there must be an excitement for God. Like David, he must say, "As the deer pants for the water brooks, so pants my soul for You, O God" (Ps. 42:1). *Second*, the preacher must have an unquenchable thirst for truth. The study of Scripture is not dreaded but joyfully anticipated. David said, "I will delight myself in

Your commandments, which I love" (Ps. 119:47). *Third,* there must be genuine love for the church. Like David and Jesus, "Zeal for Your house has eaten me up" (Ps. 69:9; John 2:17). As Paul showed his care for the church so the preacher must have a "deep concern for all the churches" (2 Cor. 11:28). *Fourth,* let the preacher develop a longing to help save the lost. Jesus came to seek and save the lost (Luke 19:10). The preacher, like the shepherd and the woman of Luke 15, must go after the sheep that is lost and search diligently for the lost coin. "He who continually goes forth weeping, bearing seed for sowing, shall doubtless come again with rejoicing, bringing his sheaves with him" (Ps. 126:6). *Fifth,* let the preacher be so filled with God's message that he can hardly wait to speak forth the oracles of God. *Sixth,* the preacher should prayerfully ask God to help him develop a passion for preaching.

SERMON PREPARATION

The preacher, first and foremost, must be a proclaimer of the Word. He is to "preach the Word" and be ready under all circumstances "to convince, rebuke, exhort with all longsuffering" (see 2 Tim. 4:1-2). How can he do this effectively?

First, let him be a student of Scripture. With or without formal training in biblical languages he can learn to do word studies by using the abundance of material available to him in lexicons, Bible dictionaries, and critical commentaries (commentaries that give the meaning and backgrounds of words). It is not a preacher's thoughts that are to be presented in teaching and preaching so much as the thoughts of Scripture. Let him allow the Scriptures to speak through him.

Second, let the preacher seek to be an expositor of Scripture. There is nothing wrong with preaching topical sermons (sermons that seek to present from various passages what the Bible says about a certain subject). However, the preaching that will best feed the congregation, contribute to the personal growth of the preacher, and bring to bear upon the hearer's mind the message of God is expository preaching. Expository preaching is to take a passage, long (several verses or a chapter) or short (a few verses), find the theme of the passage, see how it relates to the book from which it is taken (how it relates to the context), outline it to discover the flow of how the biblical author developed the theme, fill in the outline with related passages and meaningful illustrations, consider how appropriately to apply the message to the audience, saturate the preparation with prayer, study the completed outline until it becomes a part of the messenger, and present the message of truth with much love for the Lord, the Word, and the people. Even a topical sermon can be prepared and presented in that way if the preacher "exposes" the various parts of his key passages in the presentation.

Third, in sermon preparation the preacher should plan his sermons as far in advance as possible. He should keep a file folder with sermon ideas that come to his attention. He should read as many books and periodicals as he can to find these ideas. In the preacher's "additional" reading of the Bible (reading other than for sermons and class presentations) he should always be looking for sermon ideas. The preaching of a series of sermons on some book of the Bible or on some topic will help the preacher know where he is going in his preaching. The preaching of a series from a Bible book will also assure the preacher that he is preaching on a broad range of topics, as he must deal with the material that presents itself in the book. Any series of sermons should be interrupted if some special need arises in the congregation, but series preaching can be beneficial both to the preacher and to the people.

Fourth, the preacher would do well to review the sermons he has preached over the past year to make sure he is covering a broad spectrum of biblical truth in his presentations. No doubt there are some things that need to be presented more often than others, but a periodic inventory of what has been preached will assure the preacher that he is balanced in the material he presents.

Fifth, the preacher should avoid personal agendas in the preparation of his sermons. Also, he should avoid dealing specifically from the pulpit with things someone in the congregation shared with him in confidence about his personal life.

Sixth, let it be emphasized that sermon preparation should be enveloped in prayer. The preacher should pray about his preparation, the material to be used, the people who will hear, his attitude in presentation, and the desired effects the sermon will have. He should pray for insight, for wisdom, and for effective delivery.

Finally, the preacher should present "Jesus Christ and Him crucified" (1 Cor. 2:2) *in his sermons.* A good question to ask is, "How does this sermon present Christ?"

DELIVERY OF SERMONS

There are various styles used by preachers in the delivery of their sermons. Some speak from behind a pulpit stand while others walk about the pulpit. Some speak from manuscripts, some from elaborate notes, some from a few notes, and some without notes. Some speak conversationally and with few gestures while others speak with raised voices and many gestures. Whatever the style used by the preacher, it should fit his personality, and he should know his material well and seek to present it effectively. Some have suggested that for every minute used in delivering the sermon an hour should be spent in preparation. Whether or not this is correct or practical, the fact remains that sufficient time each week must be given to sermon preparation so that the sermon will be delivered with confidence and will edify the hearer. Love to study, love to discover, and love to present the message of God!

LOVE FOR TRUTH

The preacher's attitude toward Scripture will largely determine his effectiveness. The preacher must believe that the Bible is the final (Jude 3), complete (2 Tim. 3:16, 17), authoritative (1 Pet. 4:11), and inspired word of the living God (2 Pet. 1:19-21; 1 Cor. 2:13).

First, he should know the Bible teaches by words, which need to be defined, illustrated, and applied in his preaching. The words of the Old Testament were carefully preserved by the Hebrew people from the time they were written, and we are confident that the meanings of those words have remained constant through the years. As a result of this, we are sure that when we do a word study of a Hebrew word, the meaning is the same now as it was when originally written. The New Testament was written in the Koine Greek language, which was the language of the marketplace or of the common man. In the first century Koine Greek was almost a universal language, much as English is today. Over time most languages have a tendency to evolve. Many English words used in the King James Version of 1611 have different meanings today from those they had in 1611. For example, the King James Version says Christ will "judge the quick and the dead at His appearing" (2 Tim. 4:1). Today "quick" means "fast", but in 1611 it meant "living." In 1 Corinthians 16:13 the King James Version says, "Quit ye like men." To us "quit" means "stop," but in 1611 it meant "act." Words, therefore, have a tendency to evolve. However, it is interesting that while the Koine Greek language was the universal language of the first century, within a hundred or so years after the close of the first century, Greek was replaced as a universal language by Latin; therefore, the meaning of

Koine Greek words was frozen, and the language did not evolve. In a practical way this means that what a Greek word meant in the New Testament it still means today! When the preacher studies a New Testament word by using lexicons, dictionaries, and word studies, he can be confident about what a given word means as used in the New Testament. Perhaps the providence of God was at work in the freezing of the meanings of Koine Greek words!

Second, the Bible teaches by facts. When the Bible says, "In the beginning God created the heavens and the earth" (Gen. 1:1), it is a fact. When Paul affirmed that "Christ died for our sins according to the Scriptures, and that he was buried, and that He rose again the third day according to the Scriptures" (1 Cor. 15:3, 4), he presented facts.

Third, the Bible teaches by commandments. Commandments in Scripture are of two kinds: generic, or general, and specific. Sometimes God gives a commandment but does not tell us how that command should be carried out: it is generic in nature. At other times when God gives a commandment that specifies what He wants done and how He wants it carried out, it is specific. When God specifies, we must specify; when God is generic, we must be generic. It is a perversion of Scripture to treat general commandments as though they were specific or to treat specific commandments as though they were general. Perhaps an illustration will help. In Mark 16:15, 16, Jesus said, "Go into all the world and preach the gospel to every creature." "Go" we must, but the method of going is generic. Therefore, we may "go into all the world" by any means available – walking, driving an automobile, or flying in an airplane. If Christ had said, "Go into all the world on the back of a donkey," that would have been specific and we would be wonderfully hampered in our mission. However, when Jesus said, "Preach the gospel," that is specific, and we can preach no other message.

> **Seven Ways the Bible Teaches:**
> 1) Words
> 2) Facts
> 3) Commandments
> 4) Examples
> 5) Implication
> 6) Silence
> 7) Principles

Understanding the difference between generic and specific authority is very simple and fundamental but extremely important to those who love truth.

Fourth, the Bible teaches by examples. Not every action of the first-century church is binding upon us today. The time of day and the place Christians met are incidental to the fact that they did meet together. However, when an example of the early disciples has a background commandment, then what they did and how they did it should be of interest to us. For example, Jesus said in instituting the Lord's Supper, "Do this in remembrance of Me" (Luke 22:19). To obey Christ the Supper must be taken at some time. A logical question would be, "When did the early disciples do this?" Acts 20:7 says, "Upon the first day of the week." This reference is not to a common meal, which the disciples did eat later in Acts 20:11, but to the Lord's Supper. Further, people generally eat common meals every day, but Paul, although in a hurry to get to Jerusalem (Acts 20:16), stayed seven days in Troas so he could observe the Supper with them (Acts 20:6, 7). This not only indicates that the early church took the Supper on the first day of the week but that they took it only on the first day of the week. Otherwise, why did not the brethren observe it on Tuesday or Wednesday and let Paul be on his way? An action of the first-century church that has a background command becomes an example to us that should be followed. An additional note is that Acts 20:7 does not say the disciples observed the Supper every first day of the week. However, they did meet each first day (see 1 Cor. 16:1-2) for the purpose of eating the Supper (Acts 20:7). Further, when God gave the Ten Commandments, He said, "Remember the Sabbath." He did not specify every Sabbath, but Israel understood it to mean as often as the Sabbath came.

Fifth, the Bible teaches by inference or implication. An inference is a conclusion necessarily drawn from the information we have although the conclusion is not specifically stated. Remember that every command of God carries with it the authority to do whatever is necessary to carry out that command. Bible students often overlook this fact. For example, the command for the church to meet (Heb. 10:25) carries the authority to provide a place to meet. It might be under a tree, in a house, in a rented hall, or in a building provided for that purpose. The New Testament does not mention erecting buildings, but the command to meet gives the authority to provide a place. In the command to sing (Eph. 5:19) we have authority to have a song, a tune, and a songbook. When we object to adding instruments of music to worship on the grounds that the New Testament does not teach us to have them, those who would like to have instruments sometimes say, "It doesn't say to have song books either." When a songbook is used, we are doing exactly what God has asked us to do when He said, "Sing." Instrumental music is an addition to what God said, and using it is doing something different from what He said. An inference is a necessary conclusion based upon the information we have in Scripture, and instrumental music is neither a necessity nor an inference in the command to sing.

Sixth, the Bible teaches by silence. When God tells us what to do, He does not have to name everything else in the world and say, "Do not do this." God's commandments are inclusive and exclusive – they include what He says and whatever is necessary to the carrying out of what He says, and they exclude doing something else or something different from what He says.

Seventh, the Bible teaches by principle. When a need arose in the first-century church concerning material needs, the Jerusalem church members "having land sold it, and brought the money and laid it at the apostle's feet" (Acts 4:37). This was not required (see Acts 5:4), but is a principle showing how the early disciples met a need. If some catastrophe should occur today, this principle shows us how we should respond to the needs of our brethren.

Those who love truth will always consider what is stated in a text and in its context. Additionally, the question should be asked, "What did this mean to the first readers?" Then we can make application to ourselves. A conclusion drawn from a passage that would prevent it from having meaning to the first readers is probably an erroneous conclusion. Again, these are simple and fundamental matters, but they are very important to those who seek and love the truth. The preacher's love for the truth of God's word must "burn in his bones."

DEALING WITH DISCOURAGEMENT

There are factors in the life of the preacher that have a tendency to dampen the spirit and shed a negative influence upon the fire in his bones. Most of these factors involve the people with whom he works. Not everyone cares for preaching or the preacher. The preacher and his family may be unfairly criticized, or he may feel unappreciated. Any words of criticism should be placed under objective analysis to determine if there is any truth in it. The preacher should apologize for any cited misunderstandings whether he feels at fault or not. He should make adjustments in the area of criticisms and then move forward without avoiding the critic or harboring bad feelings toward him. There are times when critics must be confronted, but one will rarely win in such conflicts. One should follow the example of Jesus "who when He was reviled, did not revile in return" (1 Pet. 2:23). But a noble response won't likely lead to a lot of praise from the church; however, any praise offered should be graciously accepted. There will be many times when the preacher may feel like giving up (so did Jeremiah), but in all circumstances he should be like David, who "strengthened himself in the Lord his God" (1 Sam. 30:6)--and keep the fire burning!

THE POWER OF PREACHING

There is no doubt that preaching is not given the esteem in our times that it once enjoyed. This may be because of the kind of preaching many have heard, or it may be because of the post-modern mindset that is centered on "me." There are many who would rather sit in a group and hear themselves talk about the Bible than have someone who has done his homework present the Bible itself. Whether we like it or not, the fact remains that in many churches if something in worship is to be cut back in time, that something will be the sermon. You will have to judge why this is or whether it is legitimate. However, there is great power in effective preaching. Just notice the place that preaching occupies in Scripture! From the preaching of Noah, to the prophets, to John the Baptist, Jesus, and the apostles, preaching is paramount in the Bible. God says, "How beautiful are the feet of those who preach the gospel of peace" (Rom. 10:15).

Those who preach should never be surprised when two things happen: (1) God uses weak vessels like us to proclaim His word; (2) people's lives are changed by the proclamation of the Gospel. Good advice for the prospective preacher: Prepare carefully for preaching by study and prayer; know the people to whom you preach; stay current in illustration and application; and then boldly proclaim the word of God with a continuing fire burning in your bones!

(Chapter originally appeared in *Peaching for Passion* edited by Russell L. Dyer, Tommy F. Hayes and Jeff A. Jenkins. Printed by Clarity Publications, Oklahoma City, OK, 2005. Used by permission)

2

THE PREPARATION OF THE PREACHER

CLARENCE DELOACH

To be successful in any worthwhile endeavor demands preparation. A lawyer prepares his brief, a builder studies his plans, a farmer must study by observation or training the basics of agriculture, a doctor spends years in study and practice, and a soldier must go through basic training. Common sense demands that preparation precedes preaching.

The life of Moses demonstrates the value of preparation. God used him to accomplish great things, but God patiently trained him for the great work he was to do. God's providence worked mightily in his life. The first forty years were spent in Egypt as he was nurtured by his mother and educated by the Egyptians, but he was not ready for God's assignment. The second forty years were spent in the desert, where he was nursed by solitude and educated by God. His final forty years were used by God to lead His people through the wilderness, where he was fortified by trials, tests, and discouragements and taught by the law given by the hand of God. It has been observed that Moses spent his first forty years thinking he was somebody, the second forty years learning he was nobody, and the third forty years learning what God can do with a nobody.

Jesus called twelve ordinary men from various but ordinary walks of life. These men were given a monumental and seemingly overwhelming task. The establishment of the church and the spread of the gospel would depend upon their work. Their training would actually take place in about half the time of our Lord's ministry. But these men were vessels in divine hands. Jesus poured His life and power into them. The Holy Spirit worked through them to initiate the gospel message so that the glory and praise rests with God, not men.

The point is this: God prepared Moses, and Jesus prepared the apostles. The fact is, all of God's servants whom He used mightily in history were prepared. God's preacher today must be prepared. An older preacher gave this sage counsel to a young man who wanted to preach: "Son, prepare yourself and God will use you." But what is the nature of this preparation? There is preparation which is both general and specific.

In general, a preacher's preparation consists of all that goes into what he is — life, attitudes, and character. It is imperative that the preacher's life exemplifies the power of the gospel to change men. His conduct must be consistent with the message. While speaking the sound, healthy doctrine, he must be careful to adorn it. Paul instructed Titus, "…speak the things which are proper for sound doctrine" (Titus 2:1). The word *proper* denotes that which is fitting and appropriate. The implication is that truth requires certain conduct that reflects and is appropriate to it. In verse 10, Paul gave the reason why servants should be obedient to their masters, not with deception but in good faith, because in so doing they would *adorn* the sound doctrine. The word *adorn* is from *kosmeo*, from which our word *cosmetics* comes. It means for the Christian that the life is arranged and ordered in such a manner as to give winsomeness and attractiveness to the life. This has special significance for the gospel preacher. You cannot divorce the preacher from his preaching and you cannot separate the preacher and his life. In a sense the man is his message, the preacher is his proclamation, and the speaker is his sermon. For that very reason, Paul exhorted Timothy, "Take heed to yourself [the preacher's life] and to the doctrine [the preacher's message]. Continue in them, for in doing this you will save both yourself and those who hear you" (1 Tim. 4:16). This passage gives perspective to every true gospel preacher. In Luke's prologue to the book of Acts, he spoke of all that "Jesus began both to do and teach" (Acts 1:1). Note the order of the verbs — "do" and "teach."

THE PREACHER'S CHARACTER

For many years, the Lyman Beecher Lectureship on preaching was conducted at Yale University. Beginning in 1871 by Henry Ward Beecher, the lectureship became the greatest contribution made to the field of homiletics. In 1954, Batsell Barrett Baxter, now deceased, wrote a book entitled *The Heart of the Yale Lectures*. He summarized the best in that long series of lectures on preaching. Baxter observed, "There was no subject mentioned more often than the preacher's character."

Indeed, preaching comes to the person in the pew tinged with the life and personality of the man in the pulpit. Broadus' definition is classic: "truth through personality." When either of these ingredients is missing, the presentation cannot rightly be called preaching.

McDowell put it this way:

> You cannot give what you do not have. You cannot create consecration unless you are consecrated. You cannot cause men to do their best unless you live at your best. Learning will not do it, eloquence will not do it. Even brilliant deeds will not do it. Life giving is in the hands of life possessors.

How does the preacher's integrity translate into the reception of his message? Those who hear must see the consistency in what the preacher says and what he does. Preaching on honesty and integrity means the preacher will be honest in all business dealings, paying his bills on time. Speaking divine truth demands truthfulness in his speech, being a man of his word. The moral teaching of the Bible will be translated into the moral behavior of his daily walk. Nothing mars the influence of the preacher like immorality. The mind is to be guarded from all impurity. Paul reminded Titus, and all of us, that the grace of God that brings salvation also teaches us "that denying ungodliness and worldly lusts, we should live soberly, righteously, and godly in this present age" (Tit. 2:11, 12).

REPUTATION VS. CHARACTER

The preacher has no need to worry about his reputation as long as his character is what it should be. Reputation is what men think of us, "but all things are naked and open to the eyes of Him to whom we must give account" (Heb. 4:13). The challenge of the gospel preacher is to preach the persistent message adorned by a consistent life.

Inconsistency mars the message and causes some to minimize it. In addressing the Jews who boasted in the law, Paul said, "For the name of the God is blasphemed among the Gentiles because of you" (Rom. 2:24). The conduct of men and women in Christ that is appropriate for sound doctrine is emphasized so "that the word of God may not be blasphemed" (Tit. 2:5). Unbelievers have a field day when one of God's preachers falls into the pit of immorality. Media coverage of scandalous episodes in the lives of famous TV evangelists has caused the public to be suspicious. In recent years, more and more have been exposed for moral and ethical wrongdoing. Preachers have no immunity from the devil's exploits.

A good example and a sincere life have a greater impact in the long run than intellectual prowess or eloquence. A lecturer on preaching observed,

> In preaching it is the character of the preacher which is the preacher's power. Preaching is not a trick which can be mastered some bright morning, or a secret which can be transmitted from one man to another for a consideration...all these things, voice, gesture, rhetoric, illustration, quotations, learning, have a certain value, but they are at best superficialities, unless backed up by something better. (Jefferson)

That something better is a solid conviction and a true sincerity. One must really believe what he preaches. Paul could say, "I believe and therefore I speak" (2 Cor. 4:13). Sadly, many have continued to preach long after they have ceased to believe. A preacher who has lost his conviction about the accuracy, inerrancy, and inspiration of the Holy Scriptures would do his hearers a favor by vacating the pulpit. When the heart and mind are not in it, his preaching becomes dull, listless, and impotent. When Paul instructed Timothy concerning his work at Ephesus, he charged, "Hold fast the pattern of sound words which you have heard from me, in faith and love which are in Christ Jesus" (2 Tim. 1:13). Not only was Timothy to preach with conviction the pattern of sound words, but he was to do it with the right attitude toward God and a compassionate love toward those he taught. Paul expressed it this way, "Speaking the truth in love..." (Eph. 4:15).

There is tremendous persuasive power in sincerity. Originally, the word *sincere* denoted that which was true, genuine, the real thing. Conscientious craftsmen would advertise their wares as "sincera," that is, without wax. Deceptive artisans would take their inferior pots and other vessels and fill the cracks and flaws with wax; but when the vessels were exposed to the sun, the wax would melt and the flaws would be exposed. Sincerity creates confidence in the communicator; his convictions are somehow passed to the hearers. Older preachers referred to this phenomenon as "ethical persuasion." At no time in history have we needed preachers with clear and confident conviction more than we need them today. Our culture has become tolerant and pluralistic. When preachers absorb this world-view, their preaching becomes mere fluff and insipidness. Rather than sounding out a "thus saith the Lord," doubt, strange-sounds, half-heartedness, and pabulum have become the order of the day. Thus, pulpits have grown dull, passionless, and ineffective. Speaking with authority has been replaced with entertainment and showmanship.

Jeremiah was derided and mocked daily because he delivered the word of the Lord. God's word through him was so unpopular that he entertained thoughts of "not speaking anymore in His name." "...But His word was in my heart like a burning fire, shut up in my bones; I was weary of holding it back and I could not" (Jer. 20:7-9). God's preacher today needs that fire on the inside that motivates him to preach God's message whether men believe it or not. Paul encouraged Timothy: "Preach the word! Be ready in season and out of season. Convince, rebuke, exhort with all longsuffering and teaching" (2 Tim. 4:2).

REFERENCES

MacArthur, John. *John MacArthur's Bible Studies: The Master's Men.* Chicago: Moody Press, 1982.

Baxter, Batsell Barrett. *The Heart of the Yale Lectures.* New York: The MacMillan Co., 1954.

Broadus, John A. *The Preparation and Delivery of Sermons.* New York: Harper & Brothers, 1944.

McDowell, William Fraser. *God Ministers of Jesus Christ.* New York: The Abingdon Press, 1918.

Jefferson. *Lectures on Preaching.* quoted in *The Heart of the Yale Lectures* by Batsell B. Baxter.

3

THE PLACE OF PREACHING IN WORSHIP

JAY LOCKHART

That preaching was a part of the worship of the first century church is a well-established fact. Luke tells us that the church in Jerusalem "continued steadfastly in the apostles' doctrine and fellowship, in the breaking of bread, and in prayers" (Acts 2:42). This certainly speaks of the worship of the church where the apostles' teaching was expounded. In Antioch, Barnabas and Saul "assembled with the church and taught" for an entire year (Acts 11:26). We are told that when Paul and Barnabas were concluding their first missionary journey, they visited the churches they had planted in Asia Minor, strengthened "the souls of the disciples, exhorting them to continue in the faith," appointed "elders in every church" with prayer and fasting, and "commended them to the Lord in whom they had believed" (Acts 14:22-23). Strengthening, exhorting, appointing, praying, and commending would suggest the church in assembly; and what was done included teaching and/or preaching. Following the Jerusalem conference, Judas and Silas went to Antioch in Syria, where they "exhorted and strengthened the brethren with many words" (Acts 15:32). At Corinth Paul continued his work of preaching among the brethren for a year and six months (Acts 18:11). As he began his third missionary journey, Paul visited again the churches of Galatia and Phrygia, "strengthening all the disciples" (Acts 18:23). At Troas, where the disciples came together on the first day of the week to observe the Lord's Supper, Paul preached to the assembly (Acts 20:7). When Paul wrote his first letter to the Corinthians, one of the important aspects of the letter was the regulation of the "in church" meeting (see 1 Cor. 14:19, 28, 34, 35). The "in church" meeting took place when "the whole church comes together" for the intended purpose of worship (the letter deals with the worship of the church in Chapters 10-16), and this coming together included preaching (see 1 Cor. 14:23-40). Preaching is a part of the worship of the New Testament church.

From a practical standpoint, we are not told in Scripture how the worship assembly of the church is to unfold. We are not told the length of the preaching time, whether the sermon should come first or last or in the middle of the assembly, or who should do the preaching (except of course that it be delivered by a man - - 1 Cor. 14: 34-35; see also 1 Tim. 2:8-15). It is a matter of judgment as to whether the sermon should occupy most of the assembly time or if we should spend most of the time together in partaking of the Supper. However, it is a fact that those who do not care all that much about preaching think that it should be shorter. Traditionally, however, the sermon is allotted the most time in our assemblies. The preaching that God desires is proclamation of the Word (2 Tim. 4:1-2) which should include the "whole counsel of God" (Acts 20:27) and "Jesus Christ and Him crucified" (1 Cor. 2:1-3).

There has never been a religious revival in history that was not brought about by preaching.

Preaching in worship may be more important than many think it is. It is designed for evangelism (1 Cor. 14:24-25), the edification of the church (1 Cor. 14:26), and the glory of God (1 Pet. 4:11; 2 Thess. 1:10-12). It is the one avenue of worship in which, when faithfully performed, God speaks to us through a human spokesman. We sing to each other and to God. We pray for one another and offer our thanks and petitions to God. We commune with one another and with God. We give to God for the welfare of one another. However, it is only in the preaching of the Word that God speaks to us. With this in mind, it would seem that the church needs more preaching (more hearing of the voice of God), not less!

However, something happened to preaching on our journey to the 21st century. There was a time when the churches of Christ were the fastest growing religious group in America, when preaching was held in high esteem. Nearly all congregations had gospel meetings, lectureships, and other events that exalted preaching. We believed the Bible, we believed in the power of preaching, and we looked for opportunities to hear preaching. Our gospel meetings lasted for ten days, two weeks, and sometimes even longer. We witnessed souls saved, the erring returned, and the saved edified. Then something happened. Preaching on Sundays was pushed by some to the background and relegated to fewer than thirty minutes. Gospel meetings were reduced in length to ten days, then to a week, then to three or four days, and some congregations eliminated them altogether. Sunday sermons were reduced to shallow spiritual pep talks, preachers delivered after-dinner speeches and called them sermons, and some preachers became little more than standup comedians. Sermons lacked emphasis upon doctrine and spiritual depth and were little more than the preacher telling his congregation, "Go out there and be nice this week." Then we wondered why a generation grew up without knowing the Bible, without understanding the nature of the church, without insight into the biblical concept of worship, and without knowing how to be saved or how we should live. We forgot, or perhaps never knew, that when at least a dozen revivals occurred in the Old Testament, every one of them was brought about by preaching the word of God, that the first-century church grew by preaching, and that there has never been a religious revival in history that was not brought about by preaching. So we ceased to emphasize preaching--to our detriment--and we forgot that God made preaching a vital part of worship.

THE ESSENCE OF WORSHIP

Biblical worship is not designed to make the worshipper feel good, be entertained, or be pleased. Biblical worship is not about what we like, what we prefer, or what we think about it. The most frequently used Old Testament word for worship means "to bow down." The key New Testament word for worship means "to kiss the hand or ground toward." Our English word for worship comes from "worth-ship."

Each of these words places the emphasis where it should be — not upon self but upon the object of our worship, who is God. The term "worship" carries the idea of "reverence, homage, and respect" for God and, therefore, is about God more than it is about us.

Isaiah chapter 6 helps us see the essence of worship. When Isaiah went up to the temple that day, a day he would never forget (he noted that it was "in the year that King Uzziah died" – 6:1), he said, "I saw the Lord sitting on a throne, high and lifted up ...." First, the essence of worship includes *a proper view of God*. We will never worship correctly or get from worship what God designed we should get until we see God as He is. The seraphim cried, "Holy, holy, holy is the Lord of hosts; The whole earth is full of His glory!" (6: 2-3). God is holy, that is, He is separate from us, He is not like us, and He is above us. One of our problems is that we seek to create God in our image: we bring God down to our level and believe that He thinks, feels, and acts as we want Him to (see Isa. 55:8-9). We want to believe that since we want to worship in a certain way, since we feel a certain way, since we prefer a certain way, then God is obligated to want, to feel, and to prefer the same things we do. God is not an elderly grandfather who looks the other way when His grandchildren misbehave – He is the God of holiness who is high and lifted up. Therefore, we "serve God acceptably" when we approach Him "with reverence and godly fear" (Heb. 12:28). This God of holiness has spoken (Isa. 1:2; Heb. 1: 1-2), and His word is to be preached in worship. In hearing God's word the people are hearing the voice of God. Our worship will never be any better than our highest view of God.

Second, when the worshipper has a proper view of God, he is able to have a *proper view of himself*. When Isaiah saw the holiness of God he said,

Woe is me, for I am undone [completely exposed – JPL]!
Because I am a man of unclean lips,
And I dwell in the midst of a people of
Unclean lips;
For my eyes have seen the King,
The Lord of hosts. (6:5)

It was only after seeing the holiness of the King (the Ruler of heaven and earth), who is the Lord (YAHWEH – the One who is and was and

26

ever will be), that Isaiah saw himself as the unworthy sinner that he was.

Third, after acknowledging his sin, Isaiah is *cleansed* (6:6-7); and then, and only then, is he ready for *service* (6:8). Isaiah's cleansing and service could not take place until he saw the holiness of the Lord and until he saw the sinfulness of himself.

WORSHIP AND THE SERMON

And so it is today. In our worship God's word is preached, and in the preaching we must see the exalted Lord and our sinful selves. In response to the preached word, we seek cleansing and are then ready for service. Preaching in worship focuses on God's glory and man's need for change; and then it calls for a response. It is easy to see that God designed preaching in worship to glorify Him by the proclamation of His word — what it says, what it means, and how it applies to the hearer. Preaching is not to satisfy the hearer, to make the hearer feel good about himself, or to entertain the hearer. It is not to make us feel better but to live better. Preaching seeks not to leave the hearer where he is but to lift him towards God, to transform him, to save him, and to edify him. Preaching in worship can accomplish these goals.

As with all avenues of worship (singing, praying, the Lord's Supper, giving), preaching is *before* God and *for* people. The preacher realizes he is accountable to God for what and how he preaches. This is why, like Paul, the preacher approaches his work "in fear and in much trembling" (1 Cor. 2:3). He wants his preaching to be done well enough that he can present it to God inasmuch as he is a steward of the things of God, and "it is required in stewards that one be found faithful" (1 Cor. 4:1-2). He wants to "handle aright the word of truth" so that he may be "a worker who does not need to be ashamed" before God (2 Tim. 2:15). Further, the preacher understands that he is God's instrument, the one through whom God speaks to men. Paul said, "But we have this treasure in earthen vessels, that the excellence of the power may be of God and not of us" (2 Cor. 4:7). What an opportunity! What a responsibility! As we preach in worship, let us not take our task lightly.

4

THE PRIORITY OF PREACHING

CLARENCE DELOACH

Mark reports that "Jesus came to Galilee preaching the gospel of the Kingdom of God" (Mark 1:14). According to the prophecy of Isaiah, Jesus was anointed, "to preach the gospel to the poor, to preach deliverance to the captives, and to preach the acceptable year of the Lord" (Luke 4:17-19). But not only did Jesus come preaching, indeed, the history of God's dealing with man has been written through preaching. Noah, God's servant before the flood, was called a "preacher of righteousness" (2 Peter 2:5). Moses, a servant of God in the early history of Israel, was a prophet, literally a spokesman for God. The prophets were preachers, and now the world-wide commission calls for preaching (Matt. 28:18-20; Luke 24:47; Mark 16: 15, 16).

In the New Testament, the priority of preaching is seen in the fact that it is God's plan for creating faith in the hearer, and "without faith, it is impossible to please Him" (Heb. 11:6). In Paul's inspired treatment of how God extends His saving grace to both Jews and Gentiles, thus to the whole world, he wrote,

> For whoever calls upon the name of the Lord shall be saved. How then shall they call on Him in whom they have not believed? And how shall they believe in Him of whom they have not heard? And how shall they hear without a preacher? And how shall they

preach unless they are sent? As it is written; "How beautiful are the feet of those who preach the gospel of peace, who bring glad tidings of good things!" But they have not all obeyed the gospel; Isaiah says, 'Lord who has believed our report?" So then faith comes by hearing and hearing by the word of God. (Rom. 10: 13-17)

What a power-packed passage! It relates to the most important question as to how God saves sinful man, and it stresses the importance of preaching in the divine plan. The greatest barrier to salvation is not racial or cultural, but man's rejection of God's offer. It could be because of a refusal to receive the love of the truth so they could be saved. Or it well may be because many have not had the privilege of hearing the gospel.

An analysis of the above passage reveals the implications for preaching.

First, "whoever" calls upon the name of the Lord shall be saved. God's grace has appeared to all (Tit. 2:11), and the gospel is the power of God to salvation for everyone who believes (Rom. 1:16). God "desires all men to be saved and come to the knowledge of the truth" (1 Tim. 2:4). Peter said that God "is longsuffering toward us, not willing that any should perish but that all should come to repentance" (2 Pet. 3:9).

Second, whoever "calls upon the name of the Lord" shall be saved. The phrase, "calling upon the name of the Lord" is used often in the Old Testament to emphasize adoration and praise for His majesty and power. In the New Testament, it is used to express submissiveness to His authority and deity. In Paul's own account of his conversion, he used the phrase "calling on the name of the Lord" as a participle, expressing his obedience to the gospel, i.e., being baptized and washing away his sins (Acts 22:16). It entails all that is involved in being saved — faith, repentance, confession, and baptism for the remission of sins.

Third, "how can they call upon Him in whom they have not believed?" The desired result of genuine faith is subjection to and obedience to the object of our faith. So the order is faith, which leads to calling (obedience).

Fourth, "...how shall they believe in Him whom they have not heard?" Here the emphasis is placed upon hearing. The gospel message must be heard! The universal commission places responsibility not only upon the sounding forth of the gospel, but also upon "making disciples"

30

which implies hearing and learning that message (Matt. 28:18-20). Paul commended the Thessalonians because of the manner in which they had received the word. He said, "For this reason we also thank God without ceasing, because when you received the word of God which you heard from us, you welcomed it not as the word of men, but as it is in truth, the word of God, which also effectively works in you who believe" (2 Thess. 2:13). In their minds and hearts the hearers embraced the word even as one would welcome a friend. The word of God when accepted in this manner is powerful and effective. His word will accomplish God's divine purposes in all who believe (Isa. 55:11). When it is heard and welcomed, it can *save* (Jas. 1:18); *sanctify* (John 17:17); *mature* (I Pet. 2:2); *liberate* (John 8:31, 32); *perfect* (2 Tim. 3:16, 17); *counsel* (Ps. 119: 24); *build up* (Acts 20:32); and *give hope* (Ps. 119:147).

Fifth, "how shall they hear without a preacher?" Paul quotes from Isaiah: "How beautiful are the feet of those who preach the gospel of peace, who bring glad tidings of good things." It is the message delivered to the ends of the earth that is so beautiful. God's agenda calls for the gospel to be preached and received to bring about salvation. Salvation does not come by intuition, meditation, philosophy, tradition, mysticism, or consensus, but through hearing, believing, and obedience to the gospel of Christ.

Preaching is a vital part of God's plan. When the true preacher is content to herald God's message of the cross, though himself a "clay pot," such preaching lets God speak His own words. Thus, the preacher has the exhilarating privilege of being God's messenger. Through the process of study, he is brought into contact with the mind of the Spirit, the author of Holy Scripture. Because it is the revelation of God and His will for man, the preacher is able to speak with authority. Herein is the power of Biblical preaching. It stands to reason, therefore, that the preacher must give his heart and soul to his ministry. He is to be ready: and this readiness carries the idea of *vigilance* and *earnestness*.

5

TAKE HEED TO DOCTRINE

JAY LOCKHART

Some time ago I was having a conversation with a young preacher about preaching. In the course of our conversation, he said to me, "I'm not much on doctrine." What an amazing statement! A young man who views himself as a preacher said he was not much on doctrine. The English word "doctrine," as found in 1 and 2 Timothy and Titus, is a translation of the Greek term *didaskalia* and means "teaching." The young preacher, referenced above, was unknowingly saying he was not much on teaching! Further, he was saying that his teaching was that he was not much on teaching. What a travesty! Of course, he did not mean he was opposed to teaching, but rather that he was not much on teaching the great and fundamental doctrines of the New Testament which set apart those who are making the plea for a return to New Testament Christianity from those who are not making this plea.

In the three letters of Paul written to young preachers, Timothy and Titus, the apostle used *didaskalia* fifteen times (Young, 267). The term is used in both the active and passive voices, meaning that the word may refer to both the act of teaching and the content of the teaching (Zodhiates, 448). Paul showed the importance of teaching the right doctrine as he said there was "sound doctrine" (1 Tim. 1:10; 2 Tim. 4:3; Tit. 1:9; 2:1), "good doctrine" (1 Tim. 4:6), "the doctrine which accords with godliness" (1 Tim. 6:3), and "the doctrine of God" (Tit. 2:10; see 1 Tim. 6:1) as opposed to the teaching "that is contrary to sound doctrine" (1 Tim. 1:10), that is "the doctrines of demons" (1 Tim. 4:1), and of those who "will not endure sound doctrine" (2 Tim. 4:3). Not only did Paul set forth the truth that there is correct doctrine and incorrect teaching, but he also urged both Timothy and Titus to "charge some that they teach no other doctrine" (1 Tim. 1:3) and to "speak the things which are proper for sound doctrine" (Tit. 2:1).

Teaching the right message is never to be done in a casual way, but with diligence. Therefore, in 1 Timothy 4:16 Paul instructed Timothy: "Take heed ... to the doctrine" (*epechō*), which means "to fix the mind upon, give heed to, and pay attention to ... persevering in the acknowledgement and practice of the Christian doctrine" (Zodhiates, 617). Earlier, in 1 Timothy 4:13, Paul had said that Timothy was to "give attention to reading, to exhortation, to doctrine." To "give attention to" (*prosechē*) means to hold to "and to devote oneself to" (Zodhiates, 1231). William Mounce says that Paul was instructing Timothy to "focus his attention" on the "public reading" of Scripture, "the exhortation for the people to follow its teaching, and the doctrinal exposition of its meaning." He further explains that Timothy was "to immerse himself in the biblical text, to encourage people to follow the text, and to teach its doctrines" (Mounce, 260). This instruction to Timothy was contrasted with the empty words spoken by those who did not proclaim the "doctrine" (1 Tim. 1:7; 4:1-2). It is easy to see Paul's urgency about this matter.

WHAT IS SOUND DOCTRINE?

Sound doctrine, to which faithful teachers are to "take heed," is teaching that which is "healthy" (Zodhiates, 1402). It is to teach that which God has revealed in its "true, pure, and uncorrupted" form (Zodhiates, 1403). To teach another doctrine is to teach "contrary to sound doctrine" (1 Tim. 1:10), to reject "the words of the Lord Jesus," and to forfeit "godliness" (1 Tim. 6:3). Further, to teach some other doctrine is to fail to "hold fast the pattern of sound words" and to reject the gospel which Paul preached (2 Tim. 1:13). To "take heed ... to the doctrine" (1 Tim. 4:16) is to hold fast to what God has revealed in Scripture and to hold fast to all that God has revealed. In doing this one is preaching a sound or healthy message.

WHAT ARE THE DANGERS IN FAILING TO PREACH SOUND DOCTRINE?

As one reads 1 and 2 Timothy and Titus, he discovers that when a teacher or preacher abandons the revealed will of God, he finds that his appetite for truth gives way to error. This teacher "will not endure sound doctrine" (2 Tim. 4:3a). "Endure" translates *anexontai*, which means "they will not put up with healthy teaching" (Mounce, 574). Those who will not teach or hear the truth of God's word will follow their own ways, and the teachers will "tickle" (Mounce, 575) the "itching ears" of the hearers with "fables," messages which do not meet the standard of the gospel (see 2 Tim. 4:3-4).

Those who do not hold to sound doctrine do not understand what they say or what they affirm (1 Tim. 1:7); they teach a message that is contrary to God's word (1 Tim. 1:10); concerning faith they "have suffered shipwreck" (1 Tim. 1:19); they have departed from "the faith" (1 Tim. 4:1-2); they are proud, knowing nothing," and they are to be avoided (1 Tim. 6:3-5). Additionally, those who do not take heed to doctrine have "a form of godliness but" deny "its power" (2 Tim. 3:5). They are "always learning and never able to come to a knowledge of the truth" (2 Tim. 3:7), and they are "evil men and impostors" who are "deceiving and being deceived" (2 Tim. 3:13). To Titus, Paul spoke of people who do not teach healthy doctrine as those "whose mouths must be stopped" (Tit. 1:11), who are to be rebuked (Tit. 1:13), who "profess to know God, but in works they deny Him" (Tit. 1:16), and who are to be admonished and rejected if they refuse to be corrected (Tit. 3:10). What an indictment Paul brought against

those who would add to, take from, or change the gospel as it has been revealed by God (see Gal. 1:6-10). It is plain to see that preaching is serious business with God and places a great responsibility upon the teacher and the hearer.

HOW CAN WE TAKE HEED TO SOUND DOCTRINE?

Let us answer this question in light of what Paul had to say to Timothy and Titus with supporting statements from other parts of the New Testament.

35

1. 2 Timothy 3:14-4:5. In this passage, Paul stated that Timothy was trained in Scripture from childhood by faithful mentors (3:14-15). These mentors included his grandmother Lois and his mother Eunice. Because of this training in Scripture, Timothy had a "genuine faith" based upon the word of God (see Rom. 10:17). First, if one is to take heed to doctrine, he must be thoroughly grounded in the word of God. Second, he must believe in the power of the Word to change lives in that it is "given by inspiration of God, and is profitable [useful – JPL] for doctrine [what is right – JPL], for reproof [when one strays from what is right – JPL], for correction [how to get right – JPL], for instruction in righteousness [how to stay right – JPL]" (3:16-17). The word of God is all that one needs as he takes heed to doctrine. Third, Paul charged Timothy "before God and the Lord Jesus Christ," the one who will one day judge us all, to "preach the word" (4:1-2a). This is to be done "in season and out of season" (when people want to hear it and when they do not) (4:2b). This preaching is to "convince, rebuke, exhort, with long-suffering and teaching" (4:2c). It is to be done because some "will not endure [put up with – JPL] sound doctrine" but will accept teaching which will be contrary to the truth (4:3-4). Those who "preach the word ... sound doctrine" will be doing "the work of an evangelist" and will "fulfill [be faithful to – JPL] their ministry" (4:5).

2. 1 Timothy 4:6, 13-16; 6:14, 20. If one will give heed to doctrine, he will be "a good minister of Jesus Christ, nourished in the words of faith and of the good doctrine which" he will have "carefully followed" (4:6). Additionally, he will have paid close attention to doctrine and will teach the word upon which he has been meditating (4:13, 15). By doing this, the faithful teacher or preacher will save himself and those he teaches (4:16). Finally, the one who gives heed to doctrine will be following the commands of the Lord and will be found blameless when Christ comes again (6:14) because he has set himself to "guard" (*phulazon*: "keep watch over" – Zodhiates, 1456-57) the word that was committed to his trust (6:20).

3. 2 Timothy 1:13-14; 2:2; 4:17. The one who takes heed to doctrine will "hold fast the pattern of sound words" which he has learned from Scripture (1:13). To "hold fast" means the "continued holding" of a "lasting possession" (*eche*: Bullinger, 3780). "Pattern" is a translation of *hupotupōsin,* which means "a concise representation or form ... a pattern, example" (Zodhiates, 1430). For one to affirm that God has no patterns in the gospel is a perversion of the truth. The "good thing which was committed to you" refers to the gospel of "sound words" which God has entrusted to the care of those who would teach or preach, and this message the teacher is to "keep," i.e. "guard" (*phulazon* – see comment on 1 Tim. 6:20 above). This message is to be passed on to "faithful men who will be able to teach others also" (2 Tim. 2:2). Thus, the pattern of sound words which has been committed to the trust of faithful men is to be passed on from one generation to another. Finally, this message is to "be preached fully" (2 Tim. 4:17) by those who know and love the gospel and who take heed to doctrine.

4. 2 Timothy 2:15. One who takes heed to doctrine will be diligent to "rightly divide [handle aright: JPL] the word of truth." This means he will understand and point out to his hearers the difference between the Old Testament (the Law of Moses) and the New Testament (the Gospel of Christ). This is one of the most misunderstood concepts among religious people. Passages such as Hebrews 8:8-13, Galatians 3:16-29, Hebrews 1:1-2, Romans 7:1-7, and Ephesians 2:13-18 should be carefully studied and taught by those who preach and teach.

5. Titus 2:15; 1:1, 3, 13; 2:1,7. To Titus Paul gave the admonition to "speak ... with all authority" (2:15). Of course, all authority belongs to Christ (Matt. 28:18), and we are to hear Him (Matt. 17:5). Therefore, what Christ speaks in the gospel records is authoritative. However, the entire New Testament has the stamp of Christ's authority upon it. Paul said the things he wrote were "the commandments of the Lord" (1 Cor. 14:37), and John said that "he who knows God hears us" (1 Jn. 4:6). The New Testament is the testament of the Lord Jesus (Heb. 9:15-16). Therefore, when one teaches the New Testament, he is teaching with authority "the truth which accords with godliness" (1:1); he is teaching the word which God has "manifested ... through preaching" (1:3); he is "sound in faith" (1:13); he is speaking "the things which are proper for sound doctrine" (2:1); and he is "in doctrine showing integrity" (2:7 – *aphthorian:* "without contamination ... uncorrupted" – Zodhiates, 298). This is how the preacher and teacher are to take heed to doctrine.

CONCLUSION

What conclusions can be drawn from Paul's letters to the young preachers, Timothy and Titus? First, there is a body of inspired truth which is a pattern for all who will take heed to doctrine. Second, this pattern of inspired truth is binding upon the preacher and his hearers. Third, when one refuses to be limited to the healthy doctrine of Scripture, he gives a clear indication that he does not believe it. Fourth, since God will judge us for our preaching and teaching, let us with diligence "speak where the Bible speaks and be silent where the Bible is silent." Fifth, to pay careful attention to the teaching of Scripture is essential to the salvation of both the teacher and those being taught. Let those who teach and preach be diligent in taking heed to doctrine! Sixth, there is no more important admonition that can be given to the preacher/teacher than this: "Take heed ... to the doctrine." To do otherwise is for the preacher/teacher to place both himself and his hearers in jeopardy.

REFERENCES

Bullinger, Ethelbert W. (1976, 3rd printing), *A Critical Lexicon and Concordance to the English and Greek New Testament* (Grand Rapids: Zondervan Pub. House).

Mounce, William D. (2000), *Word Biblical Commentary, Pastoral Epistles*, Vol. 46 (Nashville: Thomas Nelson Publishers).

Young, Robert (22nd American Ed. n.d.), *Analytical Concordance to the Bible* (Grand Rapids: Wm. B. Eerdmans Publishing Company).

Zodhiates, Spiros (1992), *The Complete Word Study Dictionary: New Testament* (Iowa Falls, Iowa: Word Bible Publishers, Inc.).

(This message was first printed in *The Spiritual Sword*, "Facing the Future," Vol. 43, No. 2, January 2012, edited by Alan Highers and used here by permission)

6

THE PURPOSE OF PREACHING

CLARENCE DELOACH

Preaching is God's plan to bring sinful man into a right relationship with Him, though modern man thinks of it as antiquated and obsolete. Paul's declaration to the Corinthians puts it in perspective:

> For since, in the wisdom of God, the world through wisdom did not know God, it pleased God through the foolishness of the message preached to save those who believe. (1 Cor. 1:21)

After more than six decades, this author is still humbled when I consider the fact that God could use me, a mere clay pot, to fulfill His divine purpose in saving mankind. But it is this very fact that keeps the preacher's feet on the ground. God has used and continues to use ordinary people to accomplish extraordinary things. One of the greatest preachers of the gospel message expressed it in this manner: "But we have this treasure in earthen vessels, that the excellence of the power may be of God and not of us" (2 Cor. 4:7). The "earthen vessels" of which Paul spoke had no intrinsic value; their only worth came from the material they contained and the purpose they served. The false teachers at Corinth sought to discredit Paul as limited and weak, but

Paul acknowledged such to authenticate his ministry. In effect, he answered their charge by saying, Yes, I am just an ordinary clay pot, but I carry the priceless treasure of the glorious gospel. The treasure is not the pot, but the message it carries and proclaims.

Through history, God has been pleased to use ordinary, common, humble servants who would devote body and soul to Him. The world, then and now, has people too enamored by their own talents, intelligence, and abilities to be used effectively by God. A popular writer has observed,

> But when God chose the men through whom He would give His word to mankind, He did not choose the learned scholars of Alexandria, the distinguished philosophers of Athens, the eloquent orators of Rome, or the self-righteous leaders of Israel. He passed them all in favor of simple Galilean fisherman like Peter, John, James, and Andrew, despised traitors like Matthew, the tax collector, and obscure men like Philip, Mark, and Nathaniel. (Twelve Ordinary Men, John MacArthur, Jr., Word Publishing, Nashville, TN).

In the context of 1 Corinthians 1:18-25, the inspired Paul focused upon what he called the "foolishness of God." The philosophers at Corinth thought of the preaching of the cross as an exercise in foolishness. However, Paul contrasts the foolishness of men, which they think is wisdom, with the wisdom of God, which they think of as foolishness. The culture of the first-century Corinth was very similar to the multicultural and post-modern philosophy of the 21st century. Both view preaching as foolish and totally irrelevant to the needs of man. Modern society is captivated by the worship of science and human achievement. Man has humanized God and deified man. In our secular society, man seeks through his own efforts to learn what life is about, where and how he came to be, and what his purpose is. Any concept of a future is clouded in obscurity.

At the very heart of preaching is the love of our Creator. John stated, "We love Him, because He first loved us" (1 John 4:19). God "so loved the world that He gave His only begotten Son" (John 3:16). God desires "all men to be saved and to come to the knowledge of the truth" (1 Tim. 2:4); "For the grace of God that brings salvation has appeared to all men" (Tit. 2:11).

40

Preaching has no purpose apart from the fundamental truth that man is lost and cannot save himself. His greatest need is salvation! That does not come through self-efforts, human intelligence, or giftedness.

The preaching of the cross first makes man aware of his need, and then it provides the "good news" that can answer his need. The gospel is the "power of God" unto salvation. It reveals God's way of making man righteous (Rom. 1:16, 17), thus underscoring the need for preaching! It is not rocket science, but rather the wisdom of God.

When Paul came to Ephesus, a major city of Asia Minor, he went into the synagogue, and for three months, "he spoke boldly, reasoning and persuading concerning the things of the kingdom of God" (Acts 19: 8-10). When the opposition to his preaching increased, he entered the "school of Tyrannus," where he preached daily for two years. The historian Luke records that "all who dwelt in Asia heard the Word of the Lord Jesus, both Jews and Greeks" (Acts 19:10). At verse 20, Luke adds, "So the word of the Lord grew mightily and prevailed." The message of the gospel is both powerful and prevailing. The context reveals that the message prevailed over false religion, evil spirits, unbelief, magic, and superstition (See verses 11-19). This was the beginning of the church in Ephesus.

> *Preaching has no purpose apart from the fact that man is lost, and his greatest need is salvation from sin.*

Later, Paul would write a letter to the Ephesian church and for their benefit and ours, explain how the message preached brought about such a transition in their lives. He states, "For by grace you have been saved through faith and that not of yourselves; it is the gift of God, not of works, lest anyone should boast" (Eph. 2: 8, 9). First, they were saved by grace. The gospel is called "the word of His grace" (Acts 20:32). It is the message that proclaims God's love for the sinner and His desire to save. It is divine favor offered where there is no merit, but on the contrary much demerit. It is love given to the unlovely and unloving. This love is extended to those who don't even want it. It is seeking grace – abundant, amazing, and abounding (Rom. 5:20; 1 Tim. 1:14). God's grace embraces all that God has done in His efforts to save man. None of us could ever earn salvation. Apostolic preachers first announced what God had done before they told men what God wanted them to do. Second, they were saved through faith. Faith comes by hearing the Word of God (Rom. 10:17). Paul spoke of the "hearing of faith" (Gal. 3:2). Faith is man's response to God's grace! It embraces his believing and obeying the gospel preached. Third, it was not of works, i.e. human activity, which would cause boasting. There is no human merit in God's way of salvation. When one is "obedient to the faith," there is no reason to boast, but every reason to be eternally grateful for the mercy received (Rom. 1:5; 16:26; 1 Tim. 1:12-15).

The Ephesian Christians who were "saved by grace through faith" and "made alive" in Christ are described as having been:

1. *Dead* in trespasses and sins (Eph. 2:1). Man, in sin, is dead and needs life. Physically he is alive, but spiritually he is separated and estranged from God (Isa. 59:1, 2). The gospel quickens, that is, it gives life! Jesus came that we might have "life and have it more abundantly" (John 10:10).

2. *Disobedient*, "walking according to the course of this world, according to the prince of the power of the air, the spirit that works in the sons of disobedience" (Eph. 2:2). Satan is the father of all disobedience and rebellion. Man is sinful, "for all have sinned and fallen short of the glory of God" (Rom. 3:23).

3. *Depraved*, "fulfilling the desires of the flesh and of the mind" (Eph. 2:3). By sinful practice man becomes a child of wrath.

It is an ugly picture the Holy Spirit paints of sinful, unregenerate man — *dead, disobedient,* and *depraved!* No amount of human education, cultural status, or environment can change this! There is no difference, Paul declares between Jew and Greek, rich and poor, educated and uneducated, black and white, red or brown, (Rom. 3:22) for all have sinned (3:23). It doesn't matter whether one is in a thousand-dollar suit and works on Wall Street or is in filthy rags on a back street - all are in need of the grace of God. All need to hear the preaching of the gospel!

The dead need to be made alive, the disobedient need to submit to God, and the depraved need to be purified. Only the gospel of Christ has the power to bring about those changes. By it, the Ephesians were made *alive* (Eph. 2:1, 5); *raised up* (Eph. 2:6); *redeemed* (Eph. 1:7) and *saved* (Eph. 2:8). And it all occurred because they "trusted, after they heard the word of truth, the gospel of [their] salvation" (Eph. 1:13).

Preaching has no purpose apart from the fact that man is lost, and his greatest need is salvation from sin. Human wisdom cannot understand the sin problem, and therefore it cannot conceive of man's greatest problem whether mental, social, or spiritual. The heart of man's problem is the heart.

The wisdom of man has no solution to the heart problem - thus, the need for divine revelation. The Bible reveals the ultimate meaning of life, the true nature of man, the basis of true happiness, God's solution to the sin problem, and the inward peace that results from it.

THE WISDOM OF GOD

The Corinthians were well aware of the wise philosophers among the Greeks and Romans. Paul stated, "For the word of the cross is to those who are perishing foolishness, but to us who are being saved it is the power of God" (1 Cor. 1:18). God's wisdom as seen in the cross is superior, permanent, powerful, and effective.

Herein lies the fundamental purpose of preaching. Paul's use of the phrase "the word of the cross" comprehends the fullness of the gospel message. It entails facts to be believed, commands to be obeyed, and promises to be enjoyed (1 Cor. 15: 1-4; Acts 2:38; Rom. 8:1, 2.) It embraces God's provision for man's redemption.

Sadly, modern man has no place for divine revelation. The Bible is seen as myth or a human fabrication. So much of modern pluralism still thinks of the cross as foolishness. The word Paul used for "foolishness" is the Greek *moria*, from which we get our word *moron*. Those who are captivated by their own wisdom think of the preaching of the cross as moronic, absolute nonsense. But to those who are saved, who have known its transforming power, it is indeed the work of God. God is pleased through the preaching of what the world considers foolishness, moronic, to save those who believe. The phrase "message preached" translates one word, *kerugmatos*. It does not refer to the act of proclaiming, but denotes the content that is proclaimed. So, it is not merely the act of preaching that saves, but the preaching of the cross. The simple, truthful message of the gospel can bring about a powerful revolution in a life; from darkness to light, from slavery to liberty, from despair to hope, from poverty to riches, and from death to life.

SUMMARY

Why preach? What purposes does preaching fulfill? What is God's divine plan for preaching?

1. *It is God's appointed means of declaring His own Word to man.* The gospel preacher has the awesome responsibility, and at the same time the thrilling joy, of giving voice to God. His sobering prerogative is to be sure that he is faithful to his charge.

2. *It is God's plan for creating faith in the heart of the hearer.* "Faith comes by hearing" (Rom. 10:17), and is indispensable to salvation, "for without faith it is impossible to please God" (Heb. 11:6). The gospel presents facts to be believed, namely, a) Christ died for our sins, b) He was buried, and c) He was raised on the third day. (1 Cor. 15:1-4). Faith presupposes divine revelation. God has called His preachers to deliver that message to give hearers the opportunity to respond.

3. *It is God's way of creating life in man, who is "dead in trespasses and sins"* (Eph. 2:1). Man is not saved "by works of righteousness which he has done, but according to His mercy He saved us, through the washing of regeneration and renewing of the Holy Spirit" (Tit. 3:5). The word translated "regeneration" carries the idea of new life, a new birth or renewal. Peter described the Christians to whom he wrote as "having been born again, not of corruptible seed but incorruptible, through the word of God which lives and abides forever," then added, "Now this is the word which by the gospel was preached to you" (1 Pet. 1:23, 25). Paul had begotten the Corinthians "through the gospel" he preached to them (1 Cor. 4:15). The gospel, faithfully preached, imparts life and develops life (1 Pet. 2:2).

4. *It is God's design for edifying and maturing the believer.* The new man in Christ needs to increase in the knowledge of His will, to be fruitful in every good work, and strengthened according to His glorious power (Col. 1: 9-11). From the milk at first, he graduates to the meat of the word (1 Pet. 2:2; Heb. 5:13, 14). This advancement comes only to those who love the word, hear it eagerly, and mature thereby (Matt. 5:6; 4:4). Biblical preaching sets the table of spiritual nourishment before believers.

   Paul described the balance in his ministry to the Colossians. First, to *warn* every man; man is lost and God's wrath and judgment are real. Man needs warning. Second, to teach every man; the gospel presents a Savior, tells what to do to be saved and how to live. Third, to present every man, i.e., to develop and mature each one, to present them to Christ (see Col. 1:28, 29). Preaching is God's agenda for warning, teaching, and presenting man to God.

Preaching is God's method for enabling His word to have its perfect work. God declared by His prophet Isaiah, "So shall My word be that goes forth from My mouth; It shall not return to Me void, but it shall accomplish what I please, and it shall prosper in the thing for which I sent it" (Isa. 55:11). What a great encouragement to the gospel preacher!

Perhaps no paragraph in all the Bible gets to the heart of God's work through His word more than 2 Timothy 3:15-17:

1. *It instructs in the way of salvation.* Timothy had been taught the Holy Scriptures by his mother and grandmother. The sacred writings he had known from childhood. That background made him receptive and obedient to the gospel because those scriptures "testified of Christ, that through His name, whoever believes in Him will receive remission of sins" (Acts 10:43).

2. *The scriptures are profitable for doctrine, i.e. teaching.* The word "profitable" translates the Greek *ophelimos* which means "beneficial," "effective," and "sufficient." Paul commended the Thessalonians because "when you received the word of God which you heard from us, you welcomed it not as the word of men, but as it is in truth, the word of God, which also effectively works in you who believe" (1 Thess. 2:13). The word is effective, sufficient, and profitable for doctrine. This word does not refer to the process of teaching, but to the content, the inspired instruction given. In a culture that belittles doctrine, it is the total body of divine truth that God commissions His preachers to proclaim. Not only are preachers to declare it, but they are also to "guard the good deposit entrusted to you" (2 Tim. 1:14) and "hold fast the pattern of sound words" (1:13).

3. *It is effective for reproof.* It convicts of improper conduct and false teaching. Knowing and understanding truth will expose all falsehood and misconduct, "for the word of God is living and

powerful and sharper than any two-edged sword, piercing even to the division of soul and spirit, and the joints and marrow, and is a discerner of the thoughts and intents of the heart" (Heb. 4:12). The word probes, penetrates, discerns, and convicts the hearer. It is the divine plumb-line by which every thought, deed, principle, and action is measured.

4. *It is sufficient for correction.* When we hear God's reproof in the right spirit, God provides the restoration, renewal and strength for cleansing and rejoicing. When God disciplines, He does it for our training and good (Heb. 12:11). It results in yielding the "peaceful fruit of righteousness." God's correction is always done "in gentleness, patience, and compassion, and so must those who deliver His words of correction (2 Tim. 2:25).

5. *It is all-sufficient for training in righteousness.* The word used for training or instruction translates a word that originally had to do with the bringing up of a child. It suggests the idea of nurturing and providing all that one needs to grow and mature.

6. *The inspired, inerrant scriptures are adequate to equip and enable us to meet all the demands of righteousness, "equipping for every good work."*

God has made His preachers accountable, not to an eldership, a church, and a human institution, but to God alone, who calls and empowers him to preach and who will ultimately judge him.

REFERENCE

MacArthur, John., *Twelve Ordinary Men* (Nashville, TN: Thomas Nelson, Inc., 2002).

7

PREACHING IN A POST-MODERN CULTURE

JAY LOCKHART

There is tension in this world between God and Satan, good and evil, and light and darkness. It cannot be otherwise. This tension is never passive, indifferent, or dormant. In the Garden of Eden this tension was seen in the fall of man. Throughout the Old Testament this tension was seen in the murder of Abel, in the days of Noah, in the life of Job, and in the preaching of the prophets. In the New Testament this tension was seen when Christ came into the world, confronted the world, and was crucified by the world. It was seen when the church confronted the world, and the response of the world was persecution. This tension is seen today as the church confronts the culture. The church is unlike the culture, and its mission is to change the culture (see Matt. 28:18-20). When culture is confronted, it will resist (John 3:19-21). The disciples of Jesus "are not of the world" (John.17:14) and must never conform to the world (Rom. 12:2). So, the battle rages!

WHERE ARE WE NOW?

1. In The Religious Community. In the religious community there is controversy over Scripture as to whether or not the Bible is from God, is accurate, is infallible, is the final authority in religious matters, and/or is relevant today. There is a controversy over whether or not women should assume leadership roles in the church. In some religious groups there is controversy over whether or not practicing homosexuals should be appointed to the ministry. On a late night television talk show a lady "priest" in a denominational group argued that the Bible must be "adjusted" to fulfill the desires of the culture. A California church made door-to-door visits in its community to ask this question of non-church attendees: "What would it take for you to start attending a church?" Based upon the answers given, a church was begun that practiced what the people wanted.

2. In The Churches Of Christ. In the church there are those who say the church cannot survive unless it undergoes radical change. The changes desired are not to bring us closer to Scripture but to fulfill the desires of the materialistic and secular mindset of those who demand change. A church in Houston, Texas, took a congregational vote to decide if women would serve in leadership roles. A well-known preacher in Nashville, Tennessee, said the churches of Christ had been asking through the years, "How did the first century church do things?" Lamenting over the asking of this question, he said, "We should have been asking, 'Why did the early church do the things which it did?'" This latter question is based upon the desire to move away from any specific doctrine being preached by the church and to reject any pattern in the New Testament as being bound upon us today. However, Paul said this to Timothy: "Hold to the pattern of sound words" (2 Tim. 1:13). Others in the church are saying that the churches of Christ simply comprise a denomination which traces its roots to the Stone-Campbell movement of the 19th century. These folks make light of any appeal to restore the church of the New Testament by planting the "seed" of the Kingdom, the word of God (Luke 8:11), in the hearts of people where it can germinate and produce *Christians only* and the church Jesus built. Others approach Scripture to find justification for the practice of what they already have made up their minds to believe. Many in the church no longer accept the authority of the Bible as the last word governing faith and practice.

3. In The Culture. The postmodern mind-set of our culture rejects absolute truth on any religious or moral issue except that one can be absolutely certain there are no absolutes. In this culture, truth becomes whatever one believes to be true. The one sin that remains is "intolerance" (meaning in today's world: "accept anything and everything as equally acceptable with any other point of view") toward any thought, any idea, and any action, regardless of what it is.

HOW DID WE GET TO WHERE WE ARE?

1. In The Culture. The world before the mid-1700's is called the Premodern World, in which Divine Revelation plus human reason was said to produce objective truth. The period from the mid-1700's to the mid-1900's is called the Modern World. During this period human reason plus the scientific method (observation and experimentation), it was said, would allow one to arrive at objective truth. This period was called "The Enlightenment" as man-made discoveries in his world and created inventions that increased his knowledge of the world and made his life easier. Because of this "achievement," man began to think too highly of himself and believed he could live his life without God. His attitude was, "Glory to man in the highest." Then Charles Darwin came along and explained how man arose from lower forms of life without God, and the cycle was complete. Since about 1950 we have been in what is called the Postmodern World (Arnold Toynbee, the noted British historian, was one of the first to use this term to describe the world that emerged from World War II). Postmodernism states that human reason is the standard for living and rejects objective truth, especially in morals and religion.

2. In Religion. Liberal theologians wanted to get in on the action, so they took a low view of Scripture and rejected the supernatural. Thus, they denied the verbal inspiration of Scripture, the creation account of Genesis, the Flood in Noah's day, Jonah and the great fish, the Virgin Birth of Christ, the miracles of Christ, and the bodily resurrection of Christ. The elevation of human reason dominated the seminaries, first in Europe and then in America, and theological students were handed a crippled text of Scripture. It's little wonder that the authority of Scripture has been rejected by so many. The main-stream denominations presented a watered-down message without a clear doctrinal emphasis. Having abandoned their message, these denominations began to decline, giving rise to the "Community Church" movement. This movement continues to thrive not because it has a strong doctrinal message but because it seeks to meet the "felt needs" of its adherents. Also, it appeals to the self-centered postmodern mind-set that what one believes does not matter as much as how one feels.

3. *In The Church.* In the churches of Christ there are many of us (church leaders as well as other members) who are now concerned not so much with what the Bible says, but with what they want it to say. These folks are not asking, "Where does the Bible authorize this activity?" but they are asking, "Where does the Bible say we cannot do this?" They are not asking, "What does the Bible teach?" but "What do I think or want or prefer?" To them there are few matters of faith (things clearly taught in Scripture), but almost everything is a matter of opinion and must be acceptable to God if one is sincere.

HOW CAN WE REACH POSTMODERNS?

We do not wish to "write off" an entire generation of people (the postmodern folks) as uninterested and unreachable. There are a number of things we can do as we seek to reach this generation.

1. *Be Authentic.* Postmoderns abhor hypocrisy. They think, perhaps rightly so, that many of us profess one thing and do another. We must live right, do the loving thing in relationships, and "practice what we preach." We can be gentle in how we treat others, humbly hold to what we believe the Scriptures teach, and treat others as we wish to be treated (Matt. 7:12). We can be "real" as we seek to be examples to others (1 Tim. 4:12) as the "salt of the earth" and "the light of the world" (Matt. 5:13-16).

2. *Build Relationships.* Postmoderns long for relationships. Help them "connect" with at least five people in the church who will make every effort to develop real relationships with them in informal settings. Without personal relationships they will never hear what we are trying to say.

3. *Believe in the Power of God's Word.* Postmoderns must be exposed to Scripture. God says His word is powerful to save (Rom. 1:16) and to edify (Acts 20:32). His word must be taught to all, including postmoderns, in order that it may have its effect. Shallow spiritual "pep talks" in classes and from the pulpit will not attract or keep postmoderns.

4. *Present Apologetics.* Our English word "apologetics" is derived from the New Testament Greek noun *apologia*, which is translated an "answer" (Acts 25:16) and a "defense" (Acts 22:1; Phil. 1:7, 17; 1 Cor. 9:3; 2 Tim. 4:16; 1 Pet. 3:15). We need to answer questions that people

50

may ask concerning the fundamentals of the Christian faith and defend our beliefs. We must present the best case possible for the existence and nature of the God of the Bible, for the deity and humanity of Jesus, and for the divine inspiration of the Scriptures. Having accomplished this, we need to demonstrate the authority of Scripture and show that the Bible teaches by words (which have meaning), by facts (historical happenings), by commands (specific and generic), by approved apostolic examples (actions of the first century disciples which have as their background a direct commandment of God), necessary inferences (something clearly implied, though not expressly stated), and by silence (one cannot build a teaching upon what the Bible does not say). We must give reasons for what we believe. The Bible teaches about worship and emphasizes that in every age of the world God has always instructed men how He wishes to be worshipped. All of these matters must be carefully explored and taught to all men.

5. *Doctrine.* Although there are people who resist the whole concept of doctrine, this word simply means "teaching." Whatever is taught is doctrine. If there is no doctrine, there is no teaching. "Doctrine" is a translation of the Greek noun *didaskalia*, and the New Testament speaks of "sound doctrine" (1 Tim. 1:10; 2 Tim. 4:3; Tit. 1:9; 2:1), "good doctrine" (1 Tim. 4:6), and "God's doctrines" (1 Tim. 6:1; Tit. 2:10), as opposed to "the doctrines" of men (Matt. 15:9; Col. 2:22) and "the doctrines of demons" (1 Tim. 4:1). Paul exhorted Timothy to "take heed unto . . . the doctrine" (1 Tim. 4:16). Having laid a good foundation by the presentation of apologetics, we must teach what the New Testament says about the nature of the New Testament church, how to be saved, how God wishes to be worshipped, the roles of men and women in the church, and every other subject. Every question must be answered by what the Bible says.

CONCLUSION

Postmoderns cannot be reached by people who do not faithfully live their faith or by those who refuse to develop relationships with them. Neither can they be reached by a watered down message which fails to teach "the whole counsel of God" (Acts 20:27). If we reach the people of our day with a message that simply fulfills their felt needs, with a message which avoids doctrine, with a message that implies or states that what one believes is unimportant so long as he is sincere, with a message presented without conviction or clarity, with a message that says our approach to God is all about us without considering what God desires, or with a message that excludes such biblical words as "go" and "be" and "do" and "obey," how have we really helped them in light of eternity? We cannot reach this generation for Christ if we simply tell them to be nice without teaching them how to be saved.

8

SINISTER MOTIVES FOR PREACHING

CLARENCE DELOACH

Not everyone is properly motivated to preach. Some have sinister motives. In Paul's letter to the Philippians, he mentions the fact that "Some indeed preach Christ even from envy and strife, and some also from goodwill: the former preach Christ from selfish ambition, not sincerely, supposing to add affliction to my chains" (Phil. 1:15-17). He defined two kinds of motivation for preaching: *sinister* and *sincere*. Sincere motives are out of goodwill and love. Sinister motives arise from strife, ambition, and envy.

What are some sinister motives for preaching?

1. Some love to be "upfront;" therefore the desire for prestige, the public spotlight, and self-glory appeals to them.
2. Some with a natural "gift of gab" see it as an opportunity to sway people with their gift and make what they see as "easy money."
3. Some see preaching as a work with little supervision - one where a preacher can be his "own person" without others telling him what he must do.
4. Some who are thirsty for power view preaching as a way to exercise authority and power over others.
5. Some have an unhealthy self-image or some psychological limitation, and they think of preaching as a way of overcoming these problems.

6. Some have entered into ministry to support a shallow commitment to Christianity, reasoning that preachers have no personal problems.

These kinds of sinister motives could be multiplied; but needless to say, when these motives persist, problems are compounded. The preacher's family suffers, the church is devastated and souls are lost. The stresses and strains of preaching will generally separate the wheat from the chaff in time. No doubt, there have been some who began preaching with wrong motives, but repented and by the grace of God became effective servants of Christ.

As a young preacher, I was privileged to hear the late C. E. McGaughey present a series of four lectures on preaching at Freed-Hardeman College. The year was 1962 the week of February 5-9. Brother McGaughey divided his lectures into four specific themes:

1. Ten Commandments for a Preacher
2. Ten Mistakes of Preachers
3. Ten Problems of a Preacher
4. Ten Things That Moved Paul

These lectures have been a blessing in my ministry of preaching, and I believe they should be shared with a new generation of preachers.

McGaughey observed of Paul, "Though unmoved by 'bonds and afflictions,' he was moved by other things. His unselfish and consecrated life cannot be accounted for except that there were some very strong motivating factors that moved him." Those "motivating factors" in Paul's ministry are powerful reminders to all who would "Preach the Word" in our multi-cultural and post-modern world. Let Paul be your mentor.

Brother McGaughey mentioned the following:

1. God's love moved him (Rom. 5:8; Gal. 2:20; Eph. 2:4-5; 2 Cor. 5:11; 1 John 4:19).
2. His own love for God moved him (1 Cor. 13:1-3; 1 Cor. 16:22; Rom. 8:28; Gal. 5:6; John 13:34; John 14:23, 24).
3. His gratitude moved him (1 Tim. 1:12; Rom. 7:24, 25; Luke 8:39; 2 Pet. 1:9,10; Eph. 3:8).
4. His sense of responsibility moved him (Rom. 1:14-16; 1 Cor. 9:1; Acts 20:24).

5. His concern for the lost moved him (Rom. 10:1; Rom. 9:3; Acts 16:9-10; Acts 24:24; Phil. 2:20; Luke 19:10; Matt. 23:27).

6. The knowledge that he would have to give an account moved him (Rom. 14:10; 1 Cor. 4:1-2; 1 Cor. 9:16; Acts 22: 16, 17, 19).

7. The desire to complete his task moved him (Acts 20:24; John 17:4; Rom. 15:23-24; Phil. 1:25-26; 2 Tim. 4:7, 8; Mark 13:34).

8. He realized that there is need for haste as time is brief (2 Cor. 4:16,17; Acts 20:25,29; Acts 21:13; Eph. 5:15).

9. He was moved by knowing divine help was always near (Phil. 4:5; Acts 27:23; Heb. 4:14-16; Acts 27:25; Matt. 28:20; 2 Cor. 12:9; Phil. 4:13; Eph. 3:20).

10. He was moved by the hope of reward in the world to come (1 Thess. 2:19; 1 Cor. 3:14,15; Phil. 3:10,11,20; 1 Cor. 9:25; 2 Tim. 4:8).

HUMAN AGENCY

Essentially, God has always used human agency in the revelation of His eternal purpose. Noah was called a "preacher of righteousness" (2 Pet. 2:5; Gen. 6:9). As a herald of God's message of warning and judgment, he called the ante-deluvian world to repentance. The prophets from Moses to Malachi were primarily preachers - forth-tellers of God's word to their age. The burden upon their hearts was a message from God to deliver, though it was often unpopular. Peter described their message as "the prophetic word made more sure" than even eye-witness testimony because it "never came by the will of man, but holy men of God spoke as they were moved by the Holy Spirit" (2 Pet. 1:17-21). Here is a clear affirmation of the divine inspiration of the Old Testament.

Mark records, "Jesus came to Galilee, preaching the gospel of the Kingdom of God" (Mark 1:14). Nicodemus was absolutely right when he called Jesus "a teacher come from God" (John 3:2). John introduced Him as "the Word, and the Word was with God, and the Word was God" (John 1:1). Indeed, He is the living Word that gives substance to the written word. Following Jesus through the gospel narratives reveals a deep reverence for the scriptures. He saw in them a divine blueprint for His mission, "for I say to you that this which is written must still be accomplished in Me" (Luke 22:37). It was according to the scriptures that He *lived, taught, died,* and *rose again*.

Jesus used the scriptures as the text for His preaching. Luke records:

> [A]s His custom was, He went into the synagogue on the Sabbath day, and stood up to read. And He was handed the book of the prophet Isaiah. And when He had opened the book, He found the place where it was written, The Spirit of the Lord is upon Me, because He has anointed Me to preach the gospel to the poor, He has sent Me to heal the brokenhearted, to preach deliverance to the captives and recovery of sight to the blind, to set at liberty those who are oppressed, to preach the acceptable year of the Lord. (Luke 4:17-19)

His ministry was one of preaching, healing, delivering, recovering, liberating – good news for fallen humanity. Luke adds that when Jesus had finished, the people "marveled at the gracious words which proceeded out of His mouth" (Luke 4:22).

Jesus used personalities and principles from the Old Testament to illustrate eternal truth. The story of Elisha and the Syrian leper, Naaman, was used not only to illustrate God's compassion, but to stress the principle of obedience (Luke 4:26, 27). In His conversation with Nicodemus, He illustrated the nature of His death by appealing to the incident of the lifting up of the brazen serpent on a pole in the wilderness (John 3:14). And when He fed the five thousand, He illustrated with a reference to the manna with which God nourished His covenant people in the wilderness. He affirmed, in that context, "I am the bread of life" (John 6:31-35).

In Jesus' preaching, He appealed to scripture for warning. He spoke of the fates of Sodom and of Tyre and Sidon and of the days of Noah to illustrate the fatal results of rejecting God's messengers and coming to repentance (See Luke 10:12-14; 17:26-30).

Our Lord saw in the inspired scriptures a weapon for defense against Satan. In the wilderness, He met the repeated attacks from the Devil with "It is written" (Matt. 4:3-11).

THE APOSTLES

When Jesus called His apostles, He said, "Follow Me, and I will make you fishers of men" (Matt. 4:19). They fished for men through preaching. Paul described the "riches of the glory of this mystery among the Gentiles which is Christ in you, the hope of glory" and then added, "Him we preach, warning every man and teaching every man in all wisdom, that we may present every man perfect in Christ Jesus" (Col. 1:27, 28).

Paul's use of "we" speaks of the apostolic band. They were preachers warning every man, teaching every man to the end that he would mature in Christ. Herein resides both the scope and the goal of preaching.

First, we *proclaim* Him. At the heart of gospel preaching is the person of Christ. The word Paul used for "preach" or "proclaim" is a word *katangello*, which means a public declaration of truth.

Second, we *warn* or *admonish*. The word *noutheteo* speaks of counsel in view of coming judgment for sin. Gospel preaching admonishes sinful men to move them to repentance.

Third, we seek *maturity* and *completion* in Christ. This is the goal of preaching Christ: first to bring the hearer to Christ for forgiveness and salvation and second to mature him in Christ. Sanctification is an ongoing process, through which one can "grow in the grace and knowledge of our Lord and Savior Jesus Christ" (2 Pet. 3:18). Peter used two words for knowledge in 2 Peter. The first is *gnosis*, which is informational, i.e. facts about Christ. The second is *epignosis*, i.e. personal knowledge that entails a personal relationship. This is a transforming knowledge that motivates our personal walk with Him. Preaching is God's way of presenting the truth that leads to faith (Rom. 10:17); and then, as that faith and knowledge grows, we mature and are made complete in Him.

9

USING THE IMAGINATION IN PREACHING

JAY LOCKHART

B y "imagination" we mean "the ability to picture in one's mind what might have been without distorting any known facts." In preaching we may use the imagination to fill in the details which are not expressly stated in the biblical text but details as they might have been. The imagination must not be used to change or contradict the information that is clearly stated in the text. "The imagination is always under the control of reality" (Whitesell, 105). So the use of imagination transcends fantasy or make believe and deals with things as they possibly could have been. The proper use of imagination can catch the attention of the hearer, broaden insights into the text, and motivate the hearer to action.

IMAGINATION AND THE INTRODUCTION TO THE SERMON

In introducing a sermon entitled "The Faith of Abraham," I said,

Imagine that you lived in Mesopotamia, the land between the rivers (the Tigris and Euphrates), modern-day Iraq, Iran, Turkey, and Syria, 2000 years before Christ. You lived among idol worshippers (Josh. 24:2), but somehow in your heart of hearts you believed there must be a true and living God who was exalted far above the gods made with the hands of men. And then one day it happened! This living God called your name and gave you a commandment: "Get out of your country, to a land that I will show you » (Gen. 12:1). Following the commandment there had been promises: "I will make you a great nation; I will bless you and make your name great;...and in you all families of the earth shall be blessed" (Gen. 12:2-3). How would you have felt? What do you suppose you would have done? Here is what Abraham did: he believed the promises...and he obeyed the command. "So Abram departed as the Lord had spoken to him" (Gen. 12:4). But, wait! There were preparations to make; business to transact; property to dispose of;...and he must tell his wife, Sarai! The conversation with Sarai may have gone something like this: "Sarai, pack up; we're moving." Sarai might have asked what any wife would want to know: "Where are we moving?" And Abraham could only answer, "I don't know...we're just moving. Pack up!" And she did! What do you think your wife would do under those circumstances? Abraham did not know where he was going...but he knew Who was going with him. And that was the beginning of Abraham's walk of faith.

In a sermon I simply entitled "The Cross of Christ," I introduced it in this way:

The procession had begun at the governor's palace and had moved slowly through the narrow streets of the city. It might have been headed by a Roman Centurion riding upon a white horse. Following the Centurion we can imagine two lines of Roman soldiers with their spears, their shields, and their helmets reflecting the rays of the morning sun. And in the midst of the soldiers were three men carrying crosses upon which they would soon die. Had we been in the crowd, which lined the narrow street, our eyes would have been drawn to one of those men: the one whose garment was soaked with the blood oozing from the wounds made by the scourging he had received the night before, the one wearing the crown of thorns in mockery of his claim to be a king.

After following the crowd to the place of execution, I described how the scene might have unfolded as I included the accusing mob, the nailing of Jesus to the cross, the darkness, and the Centurion's confession. Then I asked, "What does all of this mean?" From there I presented the major points of my sermon. (For some of the thoughts presented in this introduction I am indebted to sermon audio.com and a transcribed sermon by the late Peter Marshall.)

The introduction of a sermon must capture the attention of the audience and prepare the hearer for the main points of the sermon. Therefore, the introduction must receive much thought and preparation; it should never be slighted. Using the imagination is an excellent way to accomplish this purpose.

IMAGINATION AND THE CONCLUSION OF THE SERMON

Like the introduction to a sermon, the conclusion may be neglected by the preacher even though it is a most important part of the presentation and deserves careful thought and preparation. The conclusion is a summary of the sermon, a presentation of how the sermon can be put into practice, and a call to action on the part of the audience. It must be clear, concise, brief, and powerful. The imagination can help meet the goals of the conclusion.

> *The imagination is used in preaching to fill in the details which are not expressly stated in the biblical text but details as they might have been.*

Whitesell (116) quotes from the conclusion of a sermon on "The Crucifixion" by Joseph Parker as an illustration of how the imagination can be used to bring a sermon to a powerful conclusion:

O thou great hell, take the victory, Spirit of evil, damned from eternity, mount the central cross and mock the dead as thou hast mocked the living! The night is dark enough – no such night ever settled upon the earth before. Will the light ever shine again – is the sun clean gone forever – will the blue sky ever more kiss the green earth? All the birds are dead, their music is choked; the angels have fled away and the morning stars have dropped their sweet hymn. This is chaos with an added darkness. What is happening? Maybe God and Christ are Communing in the secret places away beyond the mountains of night – may be that this *murder* will become the world's *Sacrifice* — may be that out of this blasphemy will come a Gospel for every creature. It cannot end where it is — *that* cannot be the end of all! What will come next? We must wait.

This conclusion holds the attention of the hearer, provokes contemplation by the audience, and compels each person who receives the message to want to know more and, in the meantime, to participate in the benefits of Christ's death.

In the conclusion of a sermon I preached entitled "Is It Possible to Be Just a Christian?" I said,

Imagine a man living in the depths of China who had never heard of Christ or had ever seen a copy of the New Testament. Suppose this man obtained a New Testament in his language and, after reading the Gospel accounts of Matthew, Mark, Luke, and John, he came to believe that Jesus of Nazareth is the Son of God. Imagine further that he reads the Book of Acts and, after learning how people obeyed the gospel, finds someone who baptizes him for the forgiveness of sins. What would he become? Since the seed of the Kingdom is the word of God (Luke 8:11), would he not become exactly what people in the Book of Acts became? They simply became Christians (Acts 11:26). Suppose further that this man in China taught his friends the gospel and they became Christians. From reading the New Testament, they learned about God's desire that His people meet together for worship in local congregations, and they began to do this. What church would this be? Would it not simply be the church of the New Testament? You, too, can be only a Christian and a member of Jesus' church....

This is the active imagination for concluding the sermon.

IMAGINATION AND THE ILLUSTRATION, THE APPLICATION, AND THE EXPOSITION OF THE SERMON

The Bible overflows with illustrations for every point we make in preaching, and the imagination can fill in unwritten details as we use these illustrations. Additionally, we can imagine circumstances from daily life that will illustrate our points in preaching. The same is true in application as we ask our audience to imagine themselves doing what needs to be done in response to the message. Furthermore, we can use the imagination to picture how the first readers might have heard the original message read in their worship assembly and how they might have reacted then and in the days ahead. In a sermon entitled "The Lost Christ," based upon Luke 2: 41-50 in a series in which I preached through the Gospel of Luke, I imagined how Joseph and Mary anxiously searched for Jesus among their fellow travelers and the fears they must have experienced during the three days they searched for him after returning to Jerusalem. I imagined how Jesus found his way to the temple, how he became engaged with the teachers in the temple, and what questions he may have asked and been asked. I closed this portion of the sermon by asking the audience, "What question would you have asked; what answers could you have given in light of 1 Peter 3:15? This is using the imagination in preaching, and you can do it with satisfying results by giving some careful thought to how it can be done.

REFERENCE

Whitesell, Faris D., *Power In Expository Preaching* (Grand Rapids, MI: Fleming H. Revell Company, 1963).

10

THE POWER OF PREACHING

CLARENCE DELOACH

The writer of Hebrews affirmed, For the word of God is living and powerful, and sharper than any two-edged sword, piercing even to the division of soul and spirit, and of joints and marrow, and is a discerner of the thoughts and intents of the heart" (Heb. 4:12).

This great verse states four characteristics of the word, namely, it *lives*, it is *powerful*, it is *piercing*, and it *discerns*. The power of biblical preaching rests upon the fact that God's word is powerful. It is not the preacher's message: he merely <u>presents</u> it. Effective and able preaching implies the highest view of scripture. It is the firm conviction that the Bible is the final court of appeal in all matters relating to our relationship with God and our fellowman. Preaching the word demonstrates the firm acceptance that it is inerrant and authoritative.

PRAGMATISM

So much of the religious community approaches the Bible as a good book, but one which is subject to contemporary interpretation so as to make it relevant to our culture. Actually this pragmatic, self-centered, psychological approach has so weakened the modern perception of Christianity that it has little impact upon determining values that should change and impact lives.

Biblical preaching results in revolutionary change and reflects the solid conviction that God has met every moral and spiritual need in His inspired word. A fundamental belief of every true gospel preacher is that "all scripture is inspired of God and is profitable for teaching, for reproof, for correction, for training in righteousness; that the man of God may be adequate, equipped for every good work" (2 Tim. 3:16-17).

The power is not in the preacher, but in the message he proclaims. The thesis of the book of Romans is the underlying premise of preaching:

> For I am not ashamed of the gospel of Christ, for it is the power of God to salvation for everyone who believes, for the Jew first and also for the Greek, for in it the righteousness of God is revealed from faith to faith; as it is written, "The just shall live by faith." (Rom. 1:16, 17)

To distinguish the message and the messenger, Paul stated, "But we have this treasure in earthen vessels, that the excellence of the power may be of God and not of us" (2 Cor. 4:7). "The treasure" in this verse is the same as "this ministry" in verse one. Both of these terms describe the powerful message of the cross, "the power of God and the wisdom of God" (1 Cor. 1:24). The word Paul used for *earthen* is the Greek *ostrakinos,* which refers to a cheap, baked clay pot used to store or transport a variety of things. Paul's point was to contrast the container and the content. The container is a fragile, ordinary pot, but the content is priceless! God's agenda is to take common, ordinary people and through them to do extraordinary things. And Paul gave the reason: "that the excellence of the power may be of God and not of us."

PREACH WITH AUTHORITY

Though there is no intrinsic authority in the preacher, he can speak with authority when he is faithful to the word of God. Having given instructions for Titus to "speak the things which are proper for sound doctrine" in his ministry at Crete, Paul, at the end of the chapter said, "Speak these things, exhort and rebuke with all authority" (Tit. 2:1-15). Authority, in this passage, translates a word that refers to something that is in the proper order or place. It came to be used of an official command, directive, or injunction. When Jesus had finished the

Sermon on the Mount, "the people were astonished because He taught as one having authority and not like the scribes" (Matt. 5:28). When the proclaimer is faithful to the King's message, he has the awesome privilege of preaching with authority. His mission is not to share personal insights or opinions. He is not called to philosophize, theologize, and certainly not to entertain with words that "tickle ears" and appeal to the whims or prejudices of men (2 Tim. 4:3).

The gospel preacher must put himself aside and let God speak through him unhindered. It matters not what personality traits, experience, education, or ability he may possess; he has spiritual authority only as he is faithful to the word. His authority is not personal, ecclesiastical, intellectual, or experiential. It rests entirely upon a "thus saith the Lord."

PREACHING AND MODERN CULTURE

One reason that many moderns do not like Biblical preaching is that it rings with authority. Modern culture has become anti-authoritative. And for that reason, much of the popular preaching today is accommodative, broad-minded, entertaining, ego-building and non-confrontational. It does not offend: it disturbs no conscience, and reflects the humanistic spirit of tolerance and good feeling.

The challenge to preach the gospel truth in an age of resentment toward authority, accompanied by the exaltation of personal rights and self-expression, has never been greater. These words from Paul to the young preacher, Titus, should serve as a tonic to all gospel preachers: "these things speak and exhort and reprove with all authority" (Tit. 2:15). *Speak*, i.e., preach, announce, reveal, disclose God's will whether men like it or not, whether they receive it or reject it. *Exhort*, i.e., beseech, entreat, urge, plead, and persuade men to understand, believe and obey the truth. *Reprove*, i.e., convince and correct in an effort to bring repentance and change.

Preach with power and authority, not apology!

REFERENCES

Waddey, John Waddey. *Preaching to Preachers about Preaching*. Winona, MS: J. C. Choate Publications, 1977.

McGaughey, C. E. *Lectures on Preaching. Freed-Hardeman College Annual Bible Lectureship*. Henderson, TN, 1962.

PART 2

THE CASE FOR EXPOSITORY PREACHING

11

THE EXPLANATION

CLARENCE DELOACH

The case for expository preaching in the New Testament is clear. Paul commanded the young preachers Timothy and Titus to "preach the word" (2 Tim. 4:2) and "speak these things, exhort and rebuke with all authority" (Tit. 2:15).

Even the words in the Greek language which are translated "to preach" give a strong incentive for expository preaching. More than two dozen Greek verbs are used in the New Testament to express the richness and glory of gospel preaching. We will only consider a few.

Kerrusso is used generally to express the preaching of Jesus, the apostles, and other inspired evangelists. It is the word Paul used in his divine mandate to Timothy, "preach the word." Paul gave the ingredients involved, i.e., "convincing, rebuking and exhorting" (2 Tim. 4:2). Even the manner of doing it is emphasized: "...with all longsuffering and teaching." The Holy Spirit employed that word about fifty times in the New Testament. Thayer defines *kerrusso* thus: "to be a herald - to proclaim after the manner of a herald." The ancient herald was a messenger of the king. He had the sobering responsibility of delivering the king's message without amendment or modification. The king's words had the king's authority and, therefore, could be announced with certainty and finality. The power of gospel preaching is not in the intelligence or cleverness of the messenger, but in the authority of the message.

When Paul defined his ministry to the Colossians, he said, "I became a minister according to the stewardship from God which was given to me for you, to fulfill the word of God" (Col. 1:25). His consuming passion was not to display his giftedness, oratory, or human wisdom, but faithfully to deliver God's message. He thought of his ministry as a sacred trust, and "it is required in stewards that one be found faithful" (1 Cor. 4:2). Timothy's charge was to "preach the word" and "guard that which was entrusted to him" (1 Tim. 6:20).

Another word often used interchangeably with *kerusso* is *evangelizo*, from which our English word "evangelist" is translated. It carries with it the idea of the nature of the message delivered. It is glad tidings! It is the good news of salvation from bondage and spiritual death through Christ. While *kerusso* emphasizes the faithful proclamation of the message, *evangelizo* focuses upon the content of the message. Isaiah was inspired to write seven hundred years before Christ came, "How beautiful are the feet of those who preach the gospel of peace, who bring glad tidings of good things" (Rom. 10:15).

Another word, *martyreo*, pictures the communication of truth from first-hand eye witnesses. It is translated "bear witness" and primarily describes the preaching of the apostles who were eye and ear-witnesses of Jesus. They saw His works and heard His words; thus they could bear witness and testify of the word of His grace (Rev. 1:2; Acts 1:8). To insure, however, that they revealed the testimony accurately, they were guided into all truth by the Holy Spirit (John 16:13).

Didasko is translated generally "to teach." It describes the purpose and content of the message. Jesus used this word when He gave the great commission, and Paul used it frequently to describe Timothy's work at Ephesus (See Matthew 28:18-20 and I Tim. 6:2). It was used to express Paul's efforts at Corinth for a year and a half, "teaching the word of God among them" (Acts 18:11).

Several other words are used to explain what is involved in preaching and teaching. The word "guide" is used to express Philip's efforts to help the Ethiopian to understand what Isaiah had written about the suffering servant (Acts 8:31). In Paul's preaching journeys, he would often "reason and persuade" Acts 19:8), "explain" (Acts 18:26), "vigorously refute" (Acts 18:28), "explain and demonstrate" (Acts 17:3), "declare" (Acts 13:32), "solemnly testify" (Acts 28:23), and "open and allege" (Acts 17:3).

When Jesus encountered two disciples on the road to Emmaus on the day of His resurrection, Luke reported, "He expounded unto them in all the scriptures the things concerning Himself" (Luke 24:27). Later, when they recognized Jesus, they burned within their hearts because

Jesus "opened the scriptures" that they might comprehend the word of God (Luke 24:45).

Essentially that is what expository preaching is. It opens and expounds the scriptures so we can understand. It is an approach to preaching that gives careful attention and disciplined effort to interpret Biblically, contextually explain, and practically apply the truth of the text. It entails careful exegesis and exposition of the author's intent. It begins with, continues, and concludes with the sacred text. It demands the highest view of the Bible as the fully inspired and inerrant word of God.

MISCONCEPTIONS

Many have written off expository preaching as ineffective because they have a totally inadequate concept of what it is. It is not a devotional talk. It is not concordance preaching where many passages are collected on one topic without attention given to background or context. It is not a running commentary of words, phrases without regard to theme, order, and unity. It is not a Bible School lesson that has no organizational sequence.

True exposition seeks to explicate scripture, determining the intent of the inspired writer and applying the practical lessons to the lives of the hearers. Merrill Unger explains,

No matter what the length of the portion explained may be, if it is handled in such a way that its real and essential meaning as it existed in the mind of the particular Biblical writer and it exists in the light of the overall context of scripture and is made plain and applied to the present day needs of the hearers, it may properly be said to be expository preaching. It is emphatically not preaching about the Bible, but preaching the Bible. "What saith the Lord?" is the alpha and omega of expository preaching. It begins in the Bible and ends in the Bible, and all that intervenes springs from the Bible. In other words, expository preaching is Bible-centered preaching!

Stafford North has written,

Expository preaching is a method for finding in a passage of scripture the fundamental message the Bible writer desired to convey, capsuling that message so it can be easily grasped, and

71

elaborating on that message primarily with material from the passage itself.

Real expository preaching is doctrinal because it addresses specific truth from God to man. It is that truth that makes man free, being essential to well-being here and salvation in eternity (John 8:32). There is a cultural disdain for doctrine in our present society because man does not want a definitive and final word from God. Many want their ears tickled and their consciences soothed by vague generalities, moral platitudes, and a feel-good self-esteem. Our culture prefers spiritual junk food to a balanced diet of Biblical nutrition.

CHALLENGES

From the standpoint of the preacher, expository preaching is more demanding. It requires more systematic research and study. It entails careful exegesis, thoughtful analysis, and prayerful preparation. The reading and study necessary to be a great expositor enable the conscientious preacher to become so absorbed in the text that the message and the messenger become one. His words become spirit and life, and speech and soul unite. The reward is preaching from the overflow, and from heart to heart, rather than from a prepared script. The expository approach, when done well, will give sincerity, conviction, power, and passion to the pulpit.

The challenge of gospel preaching is to declare the glory of God. It exalts and displays His majesty. Paul wrote,

> But even if our gospel is veiled, it is veiled to those who are perishing, whose minds the god of this age has blinded, who do not believe, lest the light of the gospel of the glory of Christ, who is the image of God, should shine on them. (2 Cor. 4:4)

It is God's design through the gospel to display His glory and grace to an unbelieving world that Satan has deceived. God's way to do this is very simple. He uses those who have been enlightened, touched, and changed by the glorious gospel to deliver His message, unfolding and exposing it through words. To exposit, open, clarify, explain, and display His divine purpose is the essence of expository preaching.

The message has its setting in historical facts, i.e., the life, teaching, death, and resurrection of Christ. These great events must be set forth

72

clearly and boldly (1 Cor. 15:1-4). The message deals with God's agenda through these events to redeem sinful humanity, thus removing His wrath through the blood of the cross (Col. 1:20). It entails God's way of justifying sinful men through faith, a faith that is submissive and obedient to the will of God. This summons the preacher to expose what God has done and then to call men to respond through obedience. Such a mandate is clearly seen in the preaching of the apostles in the book of Acts.

The gospel is a message about what God seeks to accomplish in the redeemed. Through the cross, divine justice for sin was satisfied (propitiation – Rom. 3:25); we are counted righteous in Christ (justification – Rom. 5:1); and we have been forgiven and made holy (sanctification – Heb. 12:14, 15). We have become His special people created in Christ, "zealous for good works" (Eph. 2:10; Tit. 2:14). God saves us so that we may serve, for we are His workmanship. The preacher must make these great truths known through exposition of related texts.

The gospel is a message about eternal life; that life begins with abundant life here as we consecrate hearts and lives to Christ (John 10:10). It teaches us how to live in all of our relationships, and it reveals the prospects for our future. Christ in us is the "hope of glory," a hope that is "steadfast and sure" and anchors our souls (Col. 1:27; Heb. 6:19). The assurance and certainty of eternal reward must be set forth by exposition on those great texts that deal with the promises of God.

Two great challenges are constantly before the preacher. He is first, to get it right. Much sincere, open and unprejudiced study is necessary to actually get what God is saying through the text. The second challenge is to get it across, i.e., to communicate through words and illustrations so that the message is clear, interesting, and applicable to the hearers.

12

THE PREPARATION AND DELIVERY OF EXPOSITORY SERMONS

JAY LOCKHART

The importance of the preacher's preparation of his sermons is second only to the actual delivery of those sermons. Thorough preparation assures that the delivery of the sermon becomes an exciting and anticipated moment for both speaker and hearer. So, what is involved in the preparation and delivery of sermons?

PREPARATION OF LIFE

The preacher must first prepare his *life*. He comes to the pulpit "in weakness, in fear, and in much trembling" (1 Cor. 2:3) because he recognizes the power in preaching and the fact that he has the responsibility to proclaim "the whole counsel of God" (Acts 20:27). Yet, he comes to the moment of preaching knowing that he is God's spokesman. If the preacher is successful in the proclamation of God's word, he must be a person of honesty, integrity, and holy living. In short, he must practice out of the pulpit what he proclaims from the pulpit. Like Paul, the preacher must be able to say, "Imitate me, just as I also imitate Christ" (1 Cor. 11:1). The preacher is to be "an example to the believers" (1 Tim. 4:12) in his personal life. This preparation of life includes such things as living within his income and paying his bills on time, loving the church and the people who hear him preach and allowing them to know that love, being a faithful husband and father, being above reproach in his relationships with women who are not his wife, avoiding secret sins like pornography and alcohol, and dealing with the biblical text without a personal agenda. People must see the preacher as a man of God even though, like all men, he has feet of clay.

PREPARATION OF TIME

Biblical preaching takes time. Large blocks of time must be set aside each week for preparation of sermons and classes. I am well aware of the fact that the preacher's week makes many demands on his time and that his work week may involve sixty or seventy hours. I know he is "on call" seven days a week and there are countless good things he must do beyond his preparation to preach and teach. However, the preacher should understand that his primary responsibility is preaching. He does need time for other things: family, relaxation, visitation, weddings, funerals, and congregational emergencies. But he does not need to do anything and everything he might be asked to do. I strongly believe in the preacher's keeping a list of things which need to be done on a daily and weekly basis, and the list should be prioritized: what must be done, what needs to be done, and what might be done. That list should leave room for unexpected needs which arise; and it should also include what must be done, such things as a date with my wife, attending my son's ballgame or my daughter's concert, and preparing sermon and class lessons. If the preacher shares with his elders and, as he has opportunity, his congregation the need for study time, almost everyone will respect his wishes in this area. I have always practiced an "open door" policy with the churches with which I have worked. I want the people to know that I am available and that I welcome them to visit my office. However, I do not want people simply to waste my time. One fellow said to his preacher, "I had an hour to waste, and thought I would come by and waste it with you." I do not mind, in a gentle but firm way, nudging people towards the door. Also, I do not hesitate to close my door or to go to some secluded place for uninterrupted study. Preachers must have time to prepare for the divine moment of the presentation of God's truth.

PREPARATION OF HEART

The heart of the preacher is prepared by prayer, reflections, and a daily walk with God. He should be a man of prayer. In sermon preparation he prays for "clean hands and a pure heart" as he approaches the text of Scripture. He prays for wisdom and insight. He prays for the people who will hear the message. He prays for his delivery, the acceptance of the word , and the response to the sermon. Reflection, or meditation, is a must in sermon preparation. Reflection gives the sermon an opportunity to grow throughout the week before it is delivered. Reflection gives the preacher an opportunity to examine himself (2 Cor. 13:5), to "be still" and to know that the Lord is God (Ps. 46:10), and to broaden the borders of his thought processes.

PREPARATION OF THE MIND

The mind of the preacher must "be filled with the knowledge" of the Word of God (Col. 1:9). When the message of preaching is committed to writing, it must then be committed to the mind. This is real work, when properly done, but well worth the cost of the time it takes. More will be said about this in the section which follows.

PREPARATION OF THE MESSAGE

What messages will you preach next Sunday? Over the next month? Over the next year? These questions give direction to our preaching. Some preachers struggle to answer these questions. The exposition of Scripture in a series of sermons or preaching through Bible books will solve the problem. The preacher will know where he is going in preaching, and the question will not be, "What will I preach next Sunday?" but "How can I find the time to preach all that I want and need to preach?" Additionally, the preaching will be more balanced as one will preach on themes that come up in the text that he might otherwise neglect. Do not hesitate to interrupt a series if some need arises. However, it may be surprising how often the text will speak to these needs in due time. So, how does one proceed?

1. *Prayer.* As the preacher starts to develop his sermons, he should pray for wisdom to preach to the needs of people. He should also pray as he studies his sermons for insight into the biblical text, for the people who will hear the sermon, and for the effective delivery of the sermon.

2. *Select the passage.* If the preacher is preaching through a book of the Bible, he must discover the theme and meaning of the passage. If he is preaching in expository fashion on a given subject, he must select a passage that develops this subject.

3. *Read and take notes.* The passage under consideration needs to be

read and reread, ideally from different translations. While reading the text, the preacher should write down every thought which comes to mind whether or not he thinks the thought is good or that he will use it. It is a lot easier to eliminate thoughts than it is to remember them if they were not written down. The text should be read in the original languages if he has this skill. Otherwise, the text should be read in an interlinear to find the emphasis of sentences. For example, the Greek New Testament is written with the key words at the beginning of a sentence for emphasis.

4. *Indentify the theme, the key thoughts, the key phrases, and the key words of the text.*

5. *Study the passage in context.* How does the passage relate to the immediate context and to the book as a whole?

6. *Explore the meaning of the key words.*

7. *Develop the outline.* Keep the outline as brief as possible, both in the number of major points to be made and in the sub-points.

8. *Illustrate the points.* Always be looking for illustrations which you can use later. Illustrations can be found in the Bible (as you read Scripture for purposes other than the preparation of sermons or classes, be looking for and write down illustrations), in your experiences, in books and magazines and newspapers (this is why the preacher must read widely), in stories you hear, and in countless other places. Remember that illustrations are not the sermon, but windows that let in the light of understanding.

9. *Apply the message.* The sermon is not complete until it has been applied. How can the hearer use this material this week to improve his life, help others, and/or help the church?

10. *Call for response.* The sermons must challenge people to act. What am I to do in response to this message?

11. *Preparing the connection.* Will you use powerpoint? Will there be handouts of the sermon outlines to be filled in by the hearers? Are you ready to speak with clarity the eternal truth of God?

12. *Approach the moment.* When all preparation has been completed, the preacher comes to the moment of presentation. He should anticipate the moment with excitement about his discoveries and the opportunity to share them with others. May God bless you as your preach the word!

13

THE APPLICATION

CLARENCE DELOACH

Advocates of liberal theology have little regard for expository preaching. The reason is obvious. Religious liberalism rejects the inerrancy of the scriptures and has chosen a more pragmatic, experience-centered approach to preaching. Stories about people and general platitudes take the place of a serious study of the text. However, the true biblical expositor reflects a clear conviction that the Bible is the verbally inspired and authoritative word of God. Because the gospel preacher sees the Bible as God's divine revelation to man, he understands that it is relevant to man's need in every culture, in all nations, and for all time. He believes the affirmation of the Psalmist, "forever, O Lord Your word is settled in heaven" (Ps. 119:89). Peter declared that the word "lives and abides forever" (1 Pet. 1:23).

Critics of expository preaching have charged that it is cold, formal, and out of touch with modern man. They claim that it does not address the concerns and issues of present society. They see it as too technical and precise for the popular mind. The question is, who decides what man needs, the Creator or the created? Is it Almighty God or man?

So much of the seeker-friendly preaching of modern times is weak and ineffective because it seeks to make the message palatable. Effort is given to providing man in his present state what he wants rather than what he needs. But it is the preacher's responsibility not to fill buildings, but to fill the pulpit with the word of God. Man, in his unregenerate state, does not know what he needs. The prophet

Jeremiah expressed it well: "O Lord, I know the way of man is not in himself; it is not in man who walks to direct his own steps" (Jer. 10:23). Awareness of this is at the heart of gospel preaching. It is the truth that brings freedom (John 8:32), but man must first recognize that he is in bondage. The gospel is the power of God to bring salvation (Rom. 1:16), but man must first understand that he is lost. The gospel is the good news of liberty and forgiveness (Eph. 1:7), but man must first be brought to recognize his slavery to sin.

Sinful man needs strength to conquer his weakness. The word of God provides revival and power. The Psalmist said, "My soul clings to the dust; revive me according to Your word" (Ps. 119:25). Man needs abiding joy, and the word of God supplies it. "Your statutes have been my songs in the house of my pilgrimage" (Ps. 119: 54). Man needs guidance, so God's word is "a lamp to my feet, and a light to my path" (Ps. 119:105). Man needs deliverance and hope. The inspired David wrote, "My soul faints for your salvation, but I hope in Your word" (Ps.s 119:81). So the satisfaction of all needs is there – in the Word!

The point is, whatever man needs, the word of God is the solution. Thus, the need for Biblical preaching! The cross of Christ is the central message of the Bible. Across the book of Genesis could be written the words, "Man needs the cross." From Exodus to Malachi there echoes the message, "The cross is coming," as it is pictured and promised. Matthew, Mark, Luke, and John reveal the "story of the cross" as Jesus' birth, life, teaching, death, and resurrection are recorded. The entire book of Acts focuses upon the "preaching of the cross" and the conversions wrought by it. The epistles describe what is entailed in "living by the cross." The book of Revelation declares the ultimate "victory through the cross."

What God has done by His amazing grace must be heralded. This is the divine mandate for preaching, "For it pleased God through the foolishness of preaching to save those who believe" (1 Cor. 1:21). God's agenda through the preaching of the gospel is "by Him to reconcile all things to Himself, by Him, whether things on earth or things in heaven, having made peace through the blood of His cross" (Col. 1:20). Man is called by the gospel, but Paul asked, "How then shall they call on Him in whom they have not believed? And how shall they believe in Him of whom they have not heard? And how shall they hear without a preacher?" (Rom. 10:14).

All of these facts give absolute relevance to Biblical preaching. John Stott has rightly observed that God's preacher today does not preach as the ancient prophets and apostles. The Word came to them by revelation. They were divinely inspired, for "holy men of God spoke as they were moved by the Holy Spirit" (2 Pet. 1:21). But in our case we must come to a knowledge and appreciation and application of the Word by thoughtful study and perspiration. Coming to the Word demands a right attitude and diligent effort. The serious expositor will come to the Word prayerfully, with the spirit of the Psalmist who implored God, "Open my eyes that I may see wondrous things from Your law" (Ps. 119:18), and "Teach me Your statutes, make me understand the way of Your precepts" (Ps. 119: 26, 27).

The effective preacher will be marked by careful and systematic observation, proper and diligent interpretation, and practical application. Observation answers the question, "What does the text say?" Interpretation answers the question, "What does the passage mean?" Application answers the question, "What does the passage mean to me, i.e., how does it relate to life?"

The Biblical expositor will ask three questions when considering a text. First, what did it mean then? Look at the text in its historical context. Second, what does the passage mean now? Make the transition from yesterday to today. And third, what does it mean to me personally? What lessons can I learn? Paul stated, "For whatever things were written before were written for our learning, that we through the patience and comfort of the scriptures might have hope" (Rom. 15:4).

The Biblical expositor must saturate his mind and heart with the Holy Scriptures. He will soon realize that a growing knowledge of the entire Bible is essential to the effective communication of any part of it. This is because the Bible possesses progress, sequence, and relatedness. Every part is related to every other part. The book of Genesis contains the germinal seed that grows and blossoms in the rest of the Bible. It cannot be overemphasized that the gospel preacher will be a skillful student, carefully interpreting, properly applying, and sincerely proclaiming the content of truth to his congregation. He will study the Bible consecutively for information, dispensationally for application, typically for illustration, doctrinally for stabilization, and devotionally for inspiration.

One of the challenges of expository preaching is to give attention to the practical principles within the text. Excellent attention could be given to the text itself - what it says in context and what it means - but unless diligent and careful thought is given to the application to real-life situations and relationships, the sermon will be staid and ineffective.

David prayed, "O Lord, incline my ear to Your testimony" (Ps. 119:36). When God speaks to us through His word, we must **listen**, for faith comes by hearing. The preacher is under obligation faithfully to deliver God's message of truth, but there is also a serious responsibility on the part of the hearer. Jesus said, "...take heed what you hear" (Mark 4:24). No communication takes place without both a giving and a receiving. In seeking to preach and hear God's truth, both the preacher and the hearer must be alert to apply the principles learned.

When the word of God is being studied, taught, or heard, the following questions will help to apply it.

1. Is there a lesson to be learned?
2. Is there a blessing here to be enjoyed?
3. Is there a command to be obeyed?
4. Is there a sin identified to be avoided?
5. Is there a truth to carry with me?
6. Is there a temptation to overcome?
7. Is there a promise to claim?
8. Is there an error to avoid?
9. Is there a false doctrine described?
10. Is there a principle or priority to live by?

These questions, when asked during the process of preparing an expository sermon, will help the preacher to apply the truth of the text to his own life and to the lives of those who hear him. Meditation is a vital part of preparation, for it enables the preacher to weave the fabric of the text into his own life. Meditation is to the soul what digestion is to the body. It nourishes the soul as food nourishes the body. Paul must have had this in mind when he challenged Timothy to be "nourished in the words of faith and of good doctrine which you have carefully followed" (1 Tim. 4:6). While moving through the word, we must allow the word to move through us.

REFERENCES

Stott, John R. W. *The Preacher's Portrait*. Grand Rapids: Eerdmans. 1961.
Moss, C. Michael. *The Exposition of Scripture, Man of God*. Nashville, TN: The Gospel Advocate Co., 1996.

14

HOW TO PREACH EXPOSITORY SERMONS

JAY LOCKHART

Something happened to preaching on the way to the 21ˢᵗ century! Preaching has always been important in God's purpose for man. From the preaching of Noah, "a preacher of righteousness" (2 Pet. 2:5) to the preaching of the Old Testament prophets to the preaching of Jesus and the apostles in the New Testament, preaching has always been prominent in God's plan. Indeed, in the New Testament era God has said, "The message of the cross is foolishness to those who are perishing, but to us who are being saved it is the power of God" (1 Cor. 1:18). Additionally, the Bible says, "(I)t pleased God through the foolishness of the message preached to save those who believe" (1 Cor. 1:21). Further, the word of God says, "For *'whoever calls on the name of the Lord shall be saved.'* How then shall they call on Him in whom they have not believed? And how shall they believe in Him of whom they have not heard? And how shall they hear without a preacher?" (Rom. 10:13-14). The church began with preaching (Acts 2), was planted throughout the Roman Empire by preaching (the Book of Acts), and was "edified" through preaching (Acts 9:26-31). Preaching was a vital part of the worship of the New Testament church (Acts 2:42; 20:7), and through preaching the lost were saved (Mark 16:15-16), and the saved were built up (Acts 20:32).

The 19th century effort to restore primitive New Testament Christianity, first in the British Isles and then in the newly established United States, came about by the preaching of the gospel . The churches of Christ were the fastest growing religious group in America in the 1950's when preaching was emphasized. However, today preaching has fallen on hard times and is no longer given the prominent place that it once occupied among us. In some churches the leaders give little opportunity for the preaching of the word. Gospel meetings are a thing of the past in these churches, sermons are little more than brief pep talks, Sunday night meetings have become pretty much social events, and as A W. Tozer observed, "The world is perishing for lack of the knowledge of God, and this church is famishing for want of His presence" (Tozer, 38).

Why has preaching been pushed to the background by many in the church? Perhaps the answer may be found in asking other questions. Do we no longer believe the message of preaching is from God? Do we believe that biblical preaching is the voice of God heard through "earthen vessels"? Have we lost confidence in the power of the word of God? Do our people see little value in the proclaimed word of God? Are we "turned off" of preaching because of the kind of preaching we have heard? Have preachers contributed to the lack of interest in preaching? Have leaders in the church allowed and encouraged this is happen? The real question we need to ask and answer is this: What can those of us who preach and leaders in the churches do about it? The partial answer is: Let us become expositors of the word, and let us support this kind of preaching with attendance, participation, and transformation!

WHAT IS PREACHING?

John A. Broadus defined preaching as "proclamation through personality." While this is not a full definition, it does emphasize the fact that preaching has to do with the message and the messenger. Two New Testament words that define preaching are *euaggelidzō*, meaning "to bring good news, to announce glad tidings" (Thayer, 256), and *kerussō*, meaning "to proclaim to persons one with whom they are to become acquainted in order to learn what they are to do" (Thayer,

346). Preaching must proclaim the good news of what God has accomplished for lost humanity through Jesus Christ. It is true that in preaching there is a time to "convince" and "rebuke" (2 Tim. 4:2), but first and foremost preaching is to announce good news. Additionally, preaching must proclaim Christ (the one with whom we are to become acquainted), and it must show hearers how to obey Christ (learn what they are to do). Biblical preaching, therefore, is to encounter God himself.

WHAT IS THE MESSAGE OF PREACHING?

Paul said to his young preacher friend, Timothy, "Preach the word" (2 Tim. 4:2). To the elders of the church at Ephesus Paul said he had "not shunned to declare to you the whole counsel of God" (Acts 20:27). To preach "the word" (*logos*) means to proclaim "the doctrine concerning the attainment through Christ of salvation in the Kingdom of God" (Thayer, 381). The word "counsel" (*boule*) is defined as "the purpose of God respecting the salvation of men through Christ...all the content of the Divine plan" (Thayer, 104, 105). To the Romans Paul said he had "fully preached the gospel of Christ" (Rom. 15:19). The term "fully" (*pleroo*) has a variety of meanings, such as "to fill, make full, fulfill, complete or finish" (O'Brien, 82). In the Roman passage, Paul may have in mind the finishing of his commission, received from the Lord, to fully take the gospel to the Gentiles. But the same root is used in Colossians 1:25 to refer to the message preached so that Gentiles might believe and obey the gospel in order that they could be presented to God "perfect in Christ" (see Col. 1:24-29). For this to be done, the full or complete gospel was preached by Paul, and it must be preached by us (see 1 Pet. 4:11 and Gal. 1:6-9). There should be no teaching of Scripture that the preacher will not preach or that he neglects to preach. The implications here are far-reaching for the preacher who fails to answer biblically the question, "What must I do to be saved?" or who never preaches on how we are to worship God, the nature and identity of the New Testament church, the role of women in the church, why we sing without mechanical accompaniment in worship, and a myriad of other basic and fundamental Bible subjects.

Further, Paul said to the Corinthians, "I determined not to know anything among you except Jesus Christ and Him crucified" (1 Cor. 2:2). When Paul said he knew nothing but Christ crucified, he was using a *synecdoche*, "a figure of speech in which a part is used for the

85

whole" (Webster, 1444). Examples of this are found in other places in the New Testament as when the first century church was "breaking bread from house to house" (Acts 2:46—clearly a reference to having a meal together; see also Acts 20:11). Also, the Lord's Supper is referred to as "to break bread" (Acts 20:7) even though the Supper included the fruit of the vine as well. The context must determine if the breaking of bread refers to the Lord's Supper or to a common meal.

Notice how inclusive the preaching of Christ and Him crucified is. First, preaching Christ crucified places the emphasis of preaching upon the message more than the messenger, which is what Paul did (see 1 Cor. 2:1-2, 3-5). Second, preaching Christ crucified focuses on man's predicament of sin since "Christ died for our sins" (1 Cor. 15:3). Third, preaching Christ crucified emphasizes the marvelous plan of God in saving us from our sins (1 Cor. 1:18). Fourth, preaching Christ crucified shows the efficacy of the blood of Christ in cleansing us from our sins (Matt. 26:28; Eph. 1:7). Fifth, preaching Christ crucified is to proclaim the "wisdom of God" which is the whole purpose and plan of God to save men and has been made known by the revelation and inspiration of the Holy Spirit (1 Cor. 2:7-13). Indeed, to preach Christ crucified includes "the whole spectrum of the inspired revelation of God, including salvation, the church, and Christian living" (Lockhart, 3-5). This is the message of preaching.

IS PREACHING RELEVANT TODAY?

In the world as well as in the church, where the value of preaching is under scrutiny, let us consider the question: "Is preaching relevant today?" Man has not changed much through the years. He may be better educated today than in the past, but his education has not satisfied the deep longings of his heart; his modern inventions and discoveries have made his life easier, but not better; what he drives and lives in have improved, but *things* never bring contentment; his standard of living rivals that of the ancient kings and queens of the earth, but *things* never bring peace of mind. Man is basically the same as he has always been; and he has ever been on a quest, whether he realized it or not, to have his greatest needs fulfilled. His greatest needs today are the same as they were yesterday. First, more than air to breathe and water to drink, man needs to be saved. The preaching of the gospel fulfills this need. The gospel is the "power of God unto salvation" (Rom. 1:16). The gospel heard, believed, obeyed, and lived brings salvation to lost men (1 Cor. 15:1-2). Second, our greatest need as Christians is to grow and mature in Christ. The preaching of the word of God will fulfill this need (1 Pet. 2:2; Acts 20:32). The preaching of the word is bread to the hungry, water to the thirsty, a compass to the sailor on the sea of life, a staff to the weary traveler on the pathway of life, and light to men in darkness. Preaching informs hearers of their responsibilities to God, convinces them of truth and error, stimulates them to proper action, and persuades them to obey the will of the Lord as God's truth is applied to specific needs. Preaching that is 1st century in content and 21st century in application will always be relevant.

HOW CAN WE BEST FULFILL THE STEWARDSHIP OF PREACHING?

As was Paul, preachers are "stewards" of the gospel of Christ (see 1 Cor. 4:1-2). A "steward" (*oikonomos*) is "the manager of a household or of household affairs" (Thayer, 440) and, therefore, "one who is overseeing something that belongs to another." Paul uses the word to speak of himself and others to whom God has entrusted the preaching of the gospel. The preacher is a steward of the word of God. Since "it is required in stewards that one be found faithful," we are asking, "How can we best fulfill the stewardship of preaching?" Here is the answer: by presenting sermons that are faithful expositions of Scripture. Let us consider a series of questions about the exposition of God's word.

1. *What are the various types of sermons?* First, there are *topical sermons*. A topical sermon has a subject and is developed by finding various passages of Scripture to support the subject. Second, there are *textual sermons*. A textual sermon is based upon a single text of Scripture in which the major points of the sermon are found, and these points may be expanded with other Scriptures. Third, there are *expository sermons*. An expository sermon is usually based upon a longer passage of Scripture and seeks to "expose" the truths that are revealed in the text. Various definitions of expository preaching have been given by students of preaching, but for our purpose I want to think of an expository sermon as one that deals with a passage of Scripture, whether the passage is long or short, in such a way as to present the setting of the passage, the theme of the passage, the title of the sermon, the thesis of the sermon, the outline of the sermon, the key thoughts of the passage, and the key words of the passage by full explanation, by

adequate illustration, and by careful application of what the passage teaches us today. It is my contention that we can best fulfill the stewardship of preaching through expository sermons. A topical sermon or a textual sermon can be presented as an expository sermon.

2. *What are the advantages of expository sermons?* First, the expository sermon allows the preacher to speak with authority. Biblical exposition is to hear the voice of God. Second, the expository sermon generates reverence for the word of God within the hearer. The message is God speaking to us. Third, the expository sermon presents the gospel as the power of God to change lives. The emphasis, then, is upon the message more than the messenger. Fourth, the expository sermon generates excitement on the part of both speaker and hearer as the deep things of God are discovered and presented. Fifth, the expository sermon challenges the preacher and the congregation to respond to the truth presented by making a decision to conform to the will of God.

Preparing Expository Sermons:

1. Select the Text
2. Study the Context
3. Read Translations
4. Continue in Prayer
5. Create a Thesis
6. Entitle the Sermon
7. Outline the Text
8. Ask questions
9. Begin and End

3. *How does the preacher prepare expository sermons?* First, a text must be selected. If the preacher is preaching a series of sermons on a certain book of the Bible, then the text is what comes next in the book. If there is a certain subject the preacher feels the congregation needs, let him find an extended passage of Scripture that deals with that subject and approach the subject with an exposition of that passage.

Second, when the text is selected, it should be read in context. Questions like, who wrote the book? to whom was it written? why was it written? should be answered in order to discover the historical background.

Third, the text should be read from several translations and, if one is skilled in the original languages, in Hebrew and/or Greek. As one reads the text, he should have pen and pad in hand so that he may write down any thought that comes to mind, whether he thinks he will later use it or not. It is a lot easier to exclude something written down than it is to remember thoughts not written down. During this process the preacher should write down the key words in the text which he will later study in detail.

Fourth, as he reads the text, the preacher should be much in prayer that the Lord will bless his studies with understanding, wisdom, and forethought as he prepares the sermon.

Fifth, after reading the text several times and writing down his thoughts, the expositor must decide what the thesis of his sermon is to be. The thesis is a one-sentence summary of what he wishes to accomplish in the sermon.

Sixth, he gives the sermon a title. He should give some thought to this so that the title itself will generate interest. Instead of giving a sermon on Psalm 51 the title, "David's Penitential Psalm," why not be a bit creative and entitle it, "When a King Was Brought to His Knees"?

Seventh, following the title the preacher needs to outline the text. The outline should be kept as simple as possible for two reasons: (1) It will help the preacher during his presentation to remember his points more easily, and (2) It will help the congregation to remember as well. Try to outline with three to five major points, depending on the text, and make an effort to use words for the major points that sound alike or begin with the same letter or contain some of the same words. Sub-points should be as brief and simple as possible so that the outline does not go beyond the main points (I,II,III, etc.), sub-points (A,B,C,etc.), and expanded points (1,2,3, etc.).

Eighth, questions should be asked about the text:

1. *The first question is, "What does it say?"* This is the easiest question to answer—it says what it says.
2. *The second question is, "What does it mean?"* Now the preacher is prepared to do some deeper study. He should discover what the words mean in the original languages by doing word studies. This will prove to be an exciting exercise as many truths begin to come to light. This is the work of **exegesis**—"to bring out the meaning of the text."
3. *The third question is, "What principles can be drawn from the text?"* This is the work of **exposition**—"to expose the teaching of the text."
4. *The fourth question is, "How does it apply to the hearer?"* This is the work of **hermeneutics**—" interpreting and applying the principles learned." Application may be the weakest link in the preparation and delivery of sermons, but until the lesson is applied, preaching has not

taken place. The application has to do with how the audience is to respond to the sermon, the action that is to be taken. Try to make sure your sermons say something to every person who hears it. This is hard work but well worth the time and effort it takes to do it well.

Six Expository Questions:

1. What does it say?
2. What does it mean?
3. What can be learned?
4. How does it apply?
5. How can it be seen?
6. Am I right?

5. *The fifth question is, "How can I illustrate the points made?"* Illustrations let in the light of understanding for the hearer. Illustrations can be found anywhere—in the Bible, in current events, in the experiences of the speaker, in what the speaker has heard, and in what the speaker has read. Illustrations can be invented by the speaker by his saying, "suppose..." or "imagine... ." The preacher should take care that he does not use an illustration about himself that did not really happen or speak as though something took place that did not.

6. Finally, the preacher should ask the question, *"What does the rest of Scripture teach about this lesson, and do my conclusions agree with the overall teaching of the Bible?"*

Ninth, when this work is done the preacher should give careful consideration to the introduction and conclusion of the sermon. The introduction, the first words he speaks, sets the tone for how the audience listens and how it participates and applies the message. Within the first minute of the presentation, the introduction must capture the attention of the hearer. The conclusion is designed to summarize the message and to call for action, and the whole sermon must lead up to the dynamic conclusion. Prayerful consideration should be given to these two elements of the sermon. (For additional information on these thoughts, see the chapter entitled, *The Preparation And Delivery of Expository Sermons*).

CONCLUSION

The preparation of expository preaching is not easy, but it is best. Both the preacher and the congregation will come to a greater appreciation for Scripture and will grow spiritually when it is done well. However, it takes a lot of time to be an expositor of the word of God. The preacher must allow large segments of time every week for preparation. Meditation, one of the requirements of the expositor, cannot be forced. As you seek to become a preacher of expository sermons, try to plan your sermons well in advance of the time of delivery. This will give them time to grow as you think about application and illustration. Preach through Bible books. Preach on topics by exposition. By doing so, you will hardly ever wonder what you will preach next. Your problem will be just how you will find time to preach everything you have planned to preach. Also, this type of preaching will allow you to be more balanced in your preaching because you will preach on themes that you might not otherwise cover. So, "preach the word" as you thoroughly prepare to be an expositor of the greatest message known to man.

REFERENCES

Lockhart, Jay, "Christ and Him Crucified," *The Spiritual Sword*, Vol. 40. No. 2, January, 2009, Alan Highers, Editor (Memphis, TN: Getwell Church of Christ, Publishers).

O'Brien, Peter T., *Word Biblical Commentary*, Vol. 44, "Colossians, Philemon" (Waco, TX: Word Books, Publishers, 1982).

Thayer, Henry, *A Greek-English Lexicon of the New Testament* (Chicago, IL.: American Book Company, n.d. reprint).

Tozer, A. W., *The Pursuit of God* (Camp Hill, PA.: Christian Publishers, Inc., 1993).

Webster's New World Dictionary (New York: Simon and Schuster, 1986 edition).

15

THE PROCESS

CLARENCE DELOACH

A MODEL FOR PREPARING EXPOSITORY SERMONS

One of the major reasons that preachers have avoided or neglected expository preaching is the challenge involved in preparation and effective presentation. With so many time restraints on the modern preacher, the discipline and effort necessary for effective exposition are often missing. But the rewards for the preacher and the congregation he serves are well worth the extra effort it entails. It encourages a more systematic and detailed study of the scriptures. Rather than taking a shot-gun approach to the Bible where scattered verses are taken and the larger body of the sermon is taken from stories, current events, and newspaper clippings, expository preaching seeks to discover and uncover the intent of the Biblical writer. It saves the preacher from becoming a specialist on one theme whether it is family concerns, current issues, apologetics, etc., though these subjects are dealt with honestly and openly when the text warrants their treatment. It keeps the preacher balanced and enables him to deal with unpopular and controversial themes as he comes to them in the text. It enables him to avoid the nervous energy spent in solving the weekly question, "What shall I preach on next Sunday?" The Bible is an inexhaustible mine of wealth. It is a stream that flows eternally. It abounds with homiletic material that no preacher can fully cover in a lifetime. And as the diligent student delves into the word, new themes will surface, and the seed will begin to germinate in the preacher's mind. As a result, themes and texts will emerge for future exposition. Every preacher should keep a list of themes and texts to develop as time and need permit.

It is the author's conviction that expository preaching will have a positive effect upon the church. It will create a solid stance regarding the scriptures, and the church needs that. The paradox of our age is a cry for education in science and technology, when the most helpful book of preparation for life and eternity is neglected. When people assert that the Bible is uninteresting and irrelevant, they are simply revealing the fact that they know very little about it. No one can deny that there is gross ignorance of the Bible in modern society, and even in the church! There can be no disputing that there is a famine of the word. But the good news is that expository preaching could reverse this trend!

The true expositor of the Word approaches the scriptures with the full understanding that it is alive and powerful. It stirs the heart, energizes the soul, and directs the life. It has the power to enlighten the mind, arouse the conscience, stir the emotions, and activate the will.

KINDS OF SERMONS

Generally, when being considered in books on homiletics, sermons are discussed under three basic categories: topical, textual, and expository. A topical sermon begins with a topic, and then numerous verses are considered that relate to the topic. A textual sermon begins with a text, normally a short one or, maybe, a single statement within the text. Then the preacher determines the major points that relate to the text. The expository approach begins with a paragraph or a larger text. It requires a careful exegesis, giving attention to the historical background. It entails the application of biblical principles of hermeneutics as the intent of the writer is determined. The points established flow from the text after which the applications are made to the hearers.

Many have asked, "What is the relationship between exegesis and exposition?" Exegesis is drawing from the text what it actually says by looking at the original language, the historical context, and the grammatical structure. Exposition, on the other hand, is displaying the truth of the text in practical and applicable ways. Nolan Howington used the following illustration to distinguish between exegesis and exposition. "Thus an exegete is like a diver bringing up pearls from the ocean bed; an expositor is like the jeweler who arrays them in orderly fashion to each other."

THE PROCEDURE

The first step is to determine the text to be treated. It could be a larger text, a paragraph, a chapter, or even a book. Remember, the theme and the points must emerge from the text. But expository sermons are not limited to an extended passage. It could be a single verse, or two or three. For example, consider James 1: 18-20. Under the theme, "The New Behavior," note the two natural points in the passage: first, the new birth (v. 18); and second, the new behavior (vs. 19-20). Under the new behavior, observe three natural points: (1.) Listen up (be swift to hear); (2.) Tone down (be slow to speak); and (3.) Sweeten up (be slow to wrath). The main emphasis is this: without the new behavior, there is no new birth.

However, the entire book of James could be used as an expository sermon on the theme, "The Behavior of Belief." For an introduction, one could show that Christianity is more than believing the right things; one must practice righteousness. The book of James is a treatise on Christianity in shoe leather, the practical side of living for Christ. Each chapter could be used to emphasize a practical faith: Chapter 1, A tried faith; Chapter 2, A working faith; Chapter 3, A controlled faith; Chapter 4, A humble faith; and Chapter 5, A praying faith.

The expository approach gives great variety to preaching. It saves the preacher from harping on one subject. It is rewarding to preach through the books of the Bible. The expository method is both intensive and extensive. It is intensive because it demands saturating one's soul in the Word of God. It enables the preacher to recognize the relatedness of all the Word. When one has preached for well over a half century, he comes to realize that some knowledge of the entire Bible is essential for the effective preaching of any part of it. The reason for this is that the Bible possesses harmony, sequence, and inter-relatedness.

Some caution needs to be exercised by anyone preparing an expository message. It is not necessary to deal with every word or subject in the passage. The details are left to the commentary, but not to the expositor. The discerning preacher can omit details that do not contribute to the theme being discussed.

THE SUBJECT – THEME

The second step in the preparation of an expository sermon is to determine the subject-theme of the text. In the third section of this book, several examples of expository sermons are given. One of them is given the theme, "A Biblical Definition of a Christian" from the text in 1 Peter 1:18 – 2:12. A reference is also given from 1 Peter 4:16, since it is one of only three times in the New Testament that the word "Christian" is used. This theme could be used as an individual sermon or as the theme of several sermons from the book of I Peter. Since Peter's use of the word "Christian" is unique to the epistles, it is only natural to assume that he would expand on the meaning of this term.

When a theme is established from a paragraph or extended text, the preacher will want to read the text in several versions and then look at commentaries, word studies, and even printed sermons that relate to the theme. Reading widely will saturate the mind with ideas and material that can be used effectively in preparation and delivery of the sermon.

THE INTRODUCTION

The introduction is extremely important to any sermon. It has been called the crucial first five minutes. In these precious moments the preacher can gain or lose his audience. He may go to great lengths to say nothing, or he may arouse the interest of his hearers for what is to follow. Briefly, the introduction should lead directly to the discussion of the text. A long tiring introduction will leave the audience loathing rather than longing. Its real purpose is to awaken an interest in the theme.

In expository preaching, there is no greater source for an introduction that the text itself. The context, with the historical setting, is an excellent way to begin. In the sermon referenced above, "A Biblical Definition of a Christian," the introduction made mention of the three references to "Christian" in the New Testament. In Acts 11:26, the first mention of "Christian," the context reveals that being a Christian entails change. In Acts 26:28, being a Christian involves choice, and in 1 Peter 4:16, being a Christian calls for challenge.

The introduction also includes a brief look at the confusion that exists in the popular mind as to what a Christian is. Some define it nationally, while others view it in terms of moral or religious affiliation.

Reference is made also to the historical context by noting in particular the persons and places addressed at the beginning of the letter.

THE DISCUSSION

The discussion is the main body of the sermon. It is that for which all the rest of the sermon exists. It is the basic structure of the presentation. Alfred Gibbs compared the sermon to a building. The preacher is the builder, and the sermon is the building he seeks to erect in the hearer's mind. He begins with a plan and then constructs the building. A foundation is first laid; then, in proper sequence, the preacher continues to build until the structure is complete.

A sermon, to be effective, must possess order, sequence, and harmony; otherwise, one may go to great length to say nothing. The major divisions should be clear and distinct. Basically, they can be stated by a series of logical statements, a series of pertinent phrases, or a series of questions. The late W. Griffith Thomas found these four elements to be a part of every effective sermon: propositions, explanations, observations, and illustrations.

Again, in the sermon "A Biblical Definition of a Christian," the main divisions are stated in a series of statements: (1.) Their relationship to God; (2.) Their redemption in Christ; and (3.) Their responsibility in life. When possible, it is good to use alliteration as a memory factor, i.e., _relationship_, _redemption_ and _responsibility_. The order and sequence follow a natural flow from the text. First, there is their _relationship_ before God as Christians (1 Pet. 1:1-5). Sub-points follow naturally: they are elect of God (1:2); begotten again (1:3); heirs of God (1:4); and preserved by God (v. 5). Second, there is their _redemption_ in Christ (1 Pet. 1:18-25). Sub-points are in sequence, beginning with the _what_ of redemption. It is not by corruptible things, but by the "precious blood of Christ" (1:19). At this point in the sermon, a Biblical study of redemption is appropriate. Other words used frequently in Romans, - i.e. "propitiation," "ransom," "justification," "adoption," and "reconciliation" - describe the riches of our salvation.

Following the nature of our redemption in Christ, Peter explores this very important question: "How were they redeemed?" What had these Christians done? Were they totally passive in their conversion? How had they responded to the gracious offer of salvation through God's grace? It is at this point in the sermon that the very crucial question of how and when redemption takes place can be emphasized from the text. Those people had believed (1:21), but was it faith alone which they manifested? They had obeyed the truth (1:22). Their faith was an active, obedient faith. Remember that those whom Peter addressed in 1 Peter, (pilgrims in Pontus, Galatia, Cappadocia, Asia, and Bithynia) were present on the day of Pentecost when Peter and the apostles preached the gospel for the first time (See Acts 2:9). They heard the message and believed (Acts 2:41) and thus were "born again by the incorruptible seed, the word of God" (1 Pet. 1:23). This is a divine commentary on Jesus' words "Unless one is born of water and the Spirit, he cannot enter the Kingdom of God" (John 3:5).

In the third part of the sermon, Peter spoke of responsibilities. A new life in Christ had begun. Peter wanted those Christians to understand that their sanctification in Christ was an on-going process. They were challenged to suffer as a Christian (1 Pet. 4:16). They were to lay aside the sins of the flesh and walk by the Spirit (1 Pet. 2:1). They were challenged to grow and mature by desiring the spiritual nourishment of the word (2:2). They were privileged to offer up worship to God as a holy priesthood (2:5). And as God's special people, they could – and must – proclaim the gospel they had received (2:9).

THE CONCLUSION

The conclusion is an appeal based upon the truth developed from the text. If one fails here, to a great extent, the message will lose its effect. On the other hand, if one succeeds at this point, he has brought home the purpose of the lesson. The conclusion should not be exhaustive or tiring.

The conclusion is not the same as the application because the application of the truth contained in the text should be made throughout the lesson. A good conclusion should be well prepared. Every sermon should be prepared and prayed over with a view to persuasion. Not every response to the gospel is made visibly. If one is lost, the preacher will want to move toward obedience and conversion. If one is wayward, the preacher strives for restoration and rededication. If one is in a saved relationship with God, the gospel preacher will motivate toward greater maturity and servant-hood.

The conclusion can be given in varied ways. A brief summary could be given with an appeal made. A good and appropriate illustration might clarify the message to the popular mind. The use of a hymn or a poem may help to bring home the message.

In the outline, "A Biblical Definition of a Christian," an appeal is made at the end based upon the simplicity of God's way of salvation. The cases of conversion in the books of Acts are consistent with and commentaries upon Peter's description of a Christian. In every case it was by "grace through faith" (Eph. 2:8). The final appeal is for hearers to do what they did and thereby become what they were – Christians (1 Pet. 4:16).

THE SUMMARY

Two great challenges stand before the preacher. First, he must get it right! That comes through sincere, open, and unprejudiced study directed toward an understanding of what God is saying in the text. Second, he must "get it across!" This entails the right words, illustrations, and applications chosen to communicate God's message with clarity and interest. The true expositor will be motivated by love for God, for His word, and for the souls of those to whom he preaches.

Every preacher has his own method of approach. Crafting the sermon is a process that requires discipline and creativity. Over time the technique can be honed and improved.

Briefly stated, the process begins by selecting a text. It could be an entire book, a chapter, a paragraph, or a verse. Here is the suggested procedure. Read the text in different translations and consult several commentaries. Observe and write down key words in the text, and research them in lexicons and word studies. Determine the central theme, and settle on an interesting title for the sermon. Write a purpose sentence or a propositional statement that summarizes the text.

Determine and state your main points that flow from the text, generally three to five. Use alliteration in stating your main points if you can, but don't force it. Settle on your sub-points and finalize your outline. A full content outline will help you preserve your research, quotations, and illustrations for further reference.

REFERENCES

Nolan Howington. "Expository Preaching." Review and Expositor 56. 1959.

Alfred P. Gibbs. The Preacher and His Preaching. Walterick Publishers. Topeka, Kansas, 1939.

Griffith Thomas, quoted in The Preacher and His Preaching. A. Gibbs. Page 215.

Harold E. Knott. How to Prepare an Expository Sermon. The Standard Publishing Foundation. Cincinnati, Ohio.

16

PREACHING EXPOSITORY SERMONS ON CHRIST AND THE CHURCH

JAY LOCKHART

It is obvious to the careful student of Scripture that New Testament preaching is centered upon Christ. The Apostle Paul, in describing his preaching at Corinth, said that he preached "the gospel...the cross of Christ" as "the power of God" to save (1 Cor. 1:17-18). He further told the Corinthians that he "determined to know" nothing while among them "except Jesus Christ and Him crucified" (1 Cor. 2:2 – For more on the meaning of this verse see THE SPIRITUAL SWORD, Vol. 40, Jan. 2009, pp. 3-5). Additionally, Paul said he preached "as of first importance" the death, burial, and resurrection of Christ (1 Cor. 15:3-4, ESV). In his second letter to the Corinthians, the apostle stated, "For we do not preach ourselves, but Christ Jesus the Lord" (2 Cor. 4:5). Paul's preaching emphasized Christ.

PREACHING IN ACTS

The preaching found in the Book of Acts follows the pattern of Paul's preaching. Peter's sermon on Pentecost proclaimed Jesus as the crucified, resurrected, and glorified Messiah who is Lord and Savior (Acts 2:22-38). Philip preached Christ to the Samaritans and to the

Ethiopian (Acts 8:5,35). The case of the Ethiopian shows that preaching Jesus includes how to be saved (Acts 8:36-39). Paul's preaching in Acts emphasized Christ. Immediately after his conversion, Paul preached "Christ...that He is the Son of God" (Acts 9:20). At Antioch in Pisidia, he preached Jesus as the one who was put to death, was buried, was raised, and was seen; as the one who fulfilled the promises God made to the fathers of Israel; and as the one who brought forgiveness and reconciliation (Acts 13:23-39). At Thessalonica, Paul preached that "Jesus...is the Christ " (Acts 17:30-33); at Corinth, the message was "Jesus is the Christ" (Acts 18:5); and at Ephesus, he preached "the word of the Lord Jesus" (Acts 19:10). When one preaches the Christ as Paul did, he is preaching the gospel (Acts 14:21), the word (Acts 15:35; 16:32; 18:11), the kingdom (Acts 20:25), and "the whole counsel of God" (Acts 20:27).

LET US PREACH CHRIST

New Testament preaching emphasized Jesus. We, too, need to preach Christ. Let us preach Christ as the promised seed of the woman (Gen. 3:15; Gal. 4:4), as the promised descendant of Abraham (Gen.12:1-7; Gal. 3:16ff.), as the Suffering Servant of prophecy (Isa. 53:1ff.; Ps. 16:10), as the eternal Word of God who became flesh and was offered up for our sins as the Lamb of God (John. 1:1-29), as God of the flesh (Jn. 1:14; Phil. 2:5-22), as the Son of God (Matt. 16:13-26; Rom. 1:4), as the greatest of teachers (Matt. 7:29), as the crucified and resurrected Savior of the world (1 Cor. 15:1-4), as the one who possesses all authority in religion (Matt. 28:18; Heb. 1:1-2), as the reigning King of kings and Lord of lords who will one day come again (1 Tim. 6:15; Heb. 1:3; Acts 2:36; Jn. 14:1-6), as the one who reigns over His established Kingdom (Mk. 9:1; Col. 1:13-14), as the one who has built His church and purchases it with His blood (Matt. 16:18; Acts 20:28), as prophet (God's spokesman to this age) and priest (the one who offered Himself to God on our behalf) and King (the Book of Hebrews), as the creator and sustainer of the universe (Heb. 1:1-2; Col. 1:16-17), as the head of the church (Eph. 1:22-23; Col. 1-18), and the final judge of all men (Matt. 25:31-46). Let us preach Christ!

LET US PREACH THE CHURCH

If one preaches Christ, it is necessary to preach about the church. This fact will be clearly seen by those who understand what the church is and who honor the teaching of the New Testament. Several years ago the expression was often heard, "Jesus, yes; church, no." This statement is still being used by some today. However, one cannot have Christ and reject the church. First, the word "church" translates the Greek term *ekklēsia*, a compound word meaning "out of" (*ek*) and "to call" (*kaleō*). The word seems to have been derived from *ekkaleÿ*, which means "the called out ones" (Zodhiates, 910). It originally referred to any called out group, but in the New Testament it is usually used in reference to the people of God, the church, who are called by the gospel out of darkness into the marvelous light of God (see 2 Th. 2:14; 1 Pet. 2:9-10). Second, the importance of the church in God's purpose is seen in that it was anticipated in Old Testament prophecy (Isa. 2:1-4; Mic. 4:1-2; 1 Tim. 3:15). Third, the establishment of the church is recorded in Acts 2 when penitent believers were baptized for the forgiveness of sins and were added to the number who were being saved (Acts 2:37-47). Therefore, the church is connected to salvation, and every person saved from sin has been added by the Lord to His church. Fourth, the church is purchased by the precious blood of Christ. Fifth, the blood of Christ *is precious* (1 Pet. 1:18-19), and that which is bought by blood is precious as well. These facts show the importance of the church and the need for preaching the truth about the church. However, there is more to be said.

THE LETTER TO THE EPHESIANS

Paul's letter to the Ephesians is an inspired portrait of the New Testament church. First, Ephesians shows that Christ has been raised from the dead by the mighty power of God, has been exalted to God's right hand where He is above all other powers, and has been made head of the church, His body (Eph. 1:20-23). Paul affirmed that Christ is the one head (He has all authority over the church) of the one body (the one church). Second, as the body of Christ, the church is the "one new man" of Ephesians 2:15 and the place where "in one body" Christ reconciles unto God all who will obey the gospel (2:16), giving members of the one body access to God (2:18). Third, as a member of Christ's body, one becomes a citizen in the Kingdom of God and has, therefore, been born again of water and the spirit, without which no one can enter the kingdom (2:19; John 3:35). If one is a part of God's kingdom, he is in God's church. Fourth, as a member of Christ's household he is, therefore, a child of God and an heir of God (Eph.

2:19; Rom. 8:17). Fifth, in the body of Christ one is a stone in the spiritual house of God, the place where God dwells (Eph. 2:20-22; 1 Pet. 2:5,9). Sixth, the church has been commissioned by God to make known to the world the plan and purpose of God in saving men (Eph. 3:8-10). Seventh, as members of the church we are to walk (live) worthy of our calling as we work for the unity of believers by proclaiming the one body, the one Spirit, the one hope, the one Lord, the one faith, the one baptism, and the one God and by every member doing his share (Eph. 4:1-6,16). This appeal for the unity of believers, based upon the teaching of the New Testament alone, is in harmony with Christ's prayer for unity (John 17:20-21) and is a clarion call for the restoration of New Testament Christianity. Eighth, members of the body of Christ are to walk in love, to walk carefully in the world (Eph. 5:1-6:24). Who can read the letter to the Ephesians and conclude that the church is optional or unimportant? After all, the church is made up of the saved people of God (Eph. 5:23). Let us preach the church.

EXPOSITORY PREACHING ON CHRIST AND THE CHURCH

How to preach expository sermons on Christ:

1. Do an exposition on "The Woman's Child" based upon Genesis 3:15; Genesis 12:1-7; Galatians 4:4; Galatians 3:16ff.
2. Give an exposition of "The Suffering Servant of Jehovah" from Isaiah 52:13-53:12. What rich material this is.
3. Preach an exposition on "The Eternal Word Who Became Flesh" based upon John 1: 1-14, 29.
4. Do an exposition on "The Mind of Christ" from Philippians 2:1-11.
5. Expose Matthew 16:13-26 on the subject of "The Identity of Jesus."
6. "Of First Importance" might be the subject of an expository sermon from 1 Corinthians 15:1-5.
7. Use Peter's outline on Pentecost as the basis of a sermon you might call, "The Christ of Scripture" (Acts 2:1-47).
8. Do an exposition of "This Present Kingdom" based upon Mark 9:1; Colossians 1:13-14; 1 Timothy 6:15.
9. Preach expositorally on "The Prophet" from Matthew 17:1; Hebrews 1:1-2; Colossians 1:16-17; Matthew 28:18; Colossians 1:18.

10. Matthew 25:31-46 could be the basis of a sermon entitled, "The Coming Lord."

HOW TO PREACH EXPOSITORY SERMONS ON THE CHURCH

In doing this, I would recommend preaching through Paul's letter to the Ephesians, a book which discloses "The Eternal Purpose of God In Christ and the Church." What a rich study that would be! For outlining and exposing the message of Ephesians see *Truth for Today Commentary*, "Ephesians and Philippians," Jay Lockhart, David L. Roper, edited by Eddie Cloer (Searcy, AR: Resource Publications), 2009. Portions of Scripture which allow the preacher to present various aspects of the church by exposition include but are not limited to the following:

1. "The Church In Prophecy" (Isa. 2:1-4; Dan. 2:44; Joel 2:28-32)
2. "Church and Kingdom" (Matt. 16:18-19; Mark 9:1; Col. 1:13-14)
3. "The beginning" (Acts 2:1-47)
4. "The Nature of the New Testament Church" (Ephesians 2:13-22)
5. "Is the Church All That Important?" (Acts 20:28; Eph. 2:16; 5:23; 1 Cor. 12:13)
6. "Finding Your Place" (1 Cor. 12:12-27)
7. "The Church in The Wilderness" (Rev. 12:1-17)
8. "Worship In Church" (1 Cor. 10:16-17; 11:17-30; 12:14-15; 14:1, 3; 16:1-2)

PREACHING TODAY

In the last several years people have lost respect for preaching. There was a time when our brethren loved preaching. We conducted gospel meetings, which lasted two weeks or longer, and large crowds attended. In our congregations, most members returned to our buildings on Sunday nights to worship and to listen to preaching. Sermons were filled with Scripture and dealt more with what people needed to hear than with what they wanted to hear. Preaching was fervent, plain, and sometimes long. People responded to the gospel, and churches of Christ were the fastest growing religious group in America. Today, things are different. Many churches have given up on gospel meetings by saying, "We can't get our members to attend." The meetings we do have are of brief duration, and sermons need to be concluded in twenty-five minutes. Additionally, sermons are often little more than

105

religious pep talks, and some preachers seem to take every opportunity to stay out of the pulpit as there is no fire in their bones for preaching (Jer. 20:9). When something needs to be shortened because of the length of the worship, the sermon usually takes the hit. Someone says, "But times are different." Of course they are, but the greatest difference between now and then may be taking place in our hearts. Have we lost our confidence in preaching? Are preachers willing to pay the price thoroughly to prepare sermons that are expositions of the word of God and to make meaningful applications to the lives of the hearers? Do we realize that whenever revivals occurred in Scripture the preaching of the word of God was always at the heart of those revivals? Do we still understand that the faithful proclamation of the word of the Lord is His power to save the lost and to edify the saved (Rom. 1:16; Acts 20:32)?

Much that is called preaching is not biblical preaching at all. Preaching that qualifies as preaching is a full exposition of the whole counsel of God by those and to those who love (2 Th. 2:10), believe (2 Th. 2:12), obey (1 Pet. 1:22), live (John 1:22), and are being transformed by the powerful word of God. Anything short of this causes the pulpit and the pew to lose respect for the proclaimed word of the Lord.

Let us restore the place of preaching in our congregations. Let us respect the word. Let us expect more of our preachers and of our congregations. Let us see the emphasis which God has always placed upon preaching. Let us acknowledge the authority of Scripture and preach it. Let us begin by preaching Christ and the church. By doing this we will come to see that preaching is more than someone standing in a pulpit and telling a congregation, "Y'all go out there and be nice this week."

REFERENCES

Zodhiates, Spiros (2nd Ed., 1992), *The Complete Word Study New Testament* (Chattanooga, TN: AMB Publishers).

(This article, in part, was first published in *The Spiritual Sword*, Volume 43, October 2011, No. 1, and is used here by permission.)

PART 3

EXAMPLES OF EXPOSITORY SERMONS

Sermons by Jay Lockhart

WHAT DOES THE LORD REQUIRE OF YOU?

(MICAH 6:6-8)

JAY LOCKHART

INTRODUCTION

A. Back in the 8th century B.C. a little boy was born into a family that lived in a small town halfway between the Dead Sea and the Mediterranean Sea. The town was called Moresheth-Gath. The little boy's parents named him Micah, a name meaning, "Who is like Yahweh," but they had no way of knowing that their boy would one day be one of God's greatest prophets. Through this prophet God would announce one of the greatest summaries of true religion ever heard and one of the finest statements of Messianic hope ever written.

B. As a prophet Micah was a contemporary of Isaiah and Hosea, and he preached in the western part of Judah a message similar to what Isaiah was preaching in Jerusalem and what Hosea was preaching in the northern kingdom of Israel.

BODY

A. The Background of Micah

1. Micah's Identity

   a) He was from Moresheth-Gath (1:1, 14) – A town on the border of Philistine near Gath; a rural area not overly impressed with the extravagance of big city living.

   b) For about 50 years Micah would speak for God, and his message would be remembered 100 years later (Jer. 26:18-19).

   c) Throughout his ministry Micah was the conscience of Israel and Judah.

2. Micah's Times
    a) Politically – Judah was threatened by Israel, who had joined Syria in her opposition to Judah, as well as the powerful Assyria. Micah spoke during the reigns of good King Jotham, the wicked Ahaz, and the wonderful Hezekiah, but the good kings could not overcome the sins of Ahaz and others, so Judah was under the judgment of God.
    b) Morally – The people, living without a consciousness of God, were characterized by greed, oppression, and violence.
    c) Religiously – The rulers were dishonest, the prophets spoke falsely, and the priests were corrupt. The people were tired of their religion (tired of God, of sacrifices, and feast days) and, while they went through the motions of serving God, their religion was a pretense because their worship was a reflection of their ungodly lives.
3. Micah's Message - There are three parts to Micah's preaching, and each section begins with "Hear...."
    a) The first section is Judgment and Promise (1:1-2:13). Following the superscription (1:1), Micah expressed God's anger with his people, the coming judgment upon them, and future deliverance. Note: God never leaves his people without hope beyond judgment.
    b) The second section is Judgment and Restoration (3:1-5:15). This section deals with the people's sin and God's retribution and the coming of the future King and his Kingdom.
    c) The third section is Judgment and Mercy (6:1-7:20). This part of Micah's message focuses on God's courtroom scene, God's reproof, and a promise for the future.

B. The Courtroom of God

1. God's Complaint (6:3-5) – God presented His case against His people with the mountains as witnesses: "What have I done to deserve the indifferent treatment I am receiving from you? Bring your charges against me."

a) God delivered them from Egypt (4).

b) God sent leaders like Moses, Aaron, and Miriam (4).

c) God gave them protection and care (5). He protected them against Balak and Balaam (see Num. 22-24). He had brought them safely through the Jordan River into the Promised Land (Acacia Grove was the last encampment before crossing the Jordan, and Gilgal was the first encampment in Canaan).

> *Note: To say that God was disappointed in his people is to use an entirely inadequate word; God was grieved and heartbroken because of their actions.*

2. The People's Response (6:6-7)

   a) The people were touched by God's complaint and sought restitution.

   b) Israel pled with God: no sacrifice will be too costly. Will God be pleased with thousands of rams or ten thousand rivers of oil? Will God be pleased with the sacrifice of our first-born children? This proposed offering of the people is comprehensive. "Burnt offerings represented total dedication. Calves a year old represented the most desirable kind of sacrificial animal. Thousands of rams and ten thousand rivers of oil represented lavish sacrifice. One's first-born represents one's most valuable possession" (Smith, *Word Biblical Commentary*, "Micah-Malachi," 51).

   c) They completely misunderstood God. God is not pleased with any outward sacrifice unless it is accompanied by hearts surrendered to Him (see Jer. **29:13**).

C. The Challenge of God

1. Here is what the Lord requires (6:8). In a careful study and application of what follows, there is some overlapping, but consider what is said in this text along with a comparison of the two New Testament texts of Titus 2:11-12 and Matthew 22:37-39.

2. "To do justly" – God wants us to *treat ourselves right*. The Hebrew word translated "justly" *(mishpāt)* is a judicial term

and speaks of justice given one in a law court (Zodhiates, *The Complete Word Study Old Testament*, 2336-2337).

  a) In Titus 2:11-12 Paul said the grace of God teaches us to live "soberly" (sōphronōs), meaning that we should be of "sound mind" (Thayer, *A Greek-English Lexicon of the New Testament*, 613) or "self-controlled" (Mounce, *Word Biblical Commentary*, "Pastoral Epistles," 424). This is to treat oneself right.

  b) In Matthew 22:37-39 Jesus said the standard by which we love our neighbor is "as yourself." It is assumed that we will love ourselves, and New Testament love is a decision to do the right thing. If we love ourselves, we will treat ourselves right. When we treat ourselves right, we will take care of our physical bodies (1 Cor. 6:19), we will control our thoughts (Phil. 4:8; 2:5), and we will seek to save our souls (Matt. 16:26).

3. "To love mercy" – God wants us to *treat others right*. The Hebrew word *(chesedh)* means the lovingkindness or mercy we choose to show to another person whether or not we have a relationship with him (Zodhiates, 2317).

  a) Titus 2:12 uses the word "righteously" *(dikaiōs)* and "emphasizes the ethical obligations" which we have toward another (Mounce, 424).

  b) Matthew 22:39 teaches us to love our neighbor.

  c) See further Matthew 7:12; James. 2:13.

4. "To walk humbly with your God" – We are to *treat God right*. If one is to walk with God, he must agree with God (see Amos 3:3).

  a) It is not so much a matter of God agreeing with us as it is that we agree with God. Since God's thoughts are not our thoughts, we must rely, not on human opinions or human reason, but upon the word of God if we are to learn what He wants us to do. Our attitude should be that of Samuel when he said, "Speak, for Your servant hears" (1 Sam. 3:10).

  b) To walk with God we need to obey God in baptism in order to walk in "newness of life" (Rom. 6:1-4). Further, we are to "walk worthy of the calling with which" we were called (Eph. 4:1ff.); we are to "walk in love" (Eph. 5:1-2); we are to "walk as children of light" (Eph. 5:1-2); and we are to "walk carefully" in the Word, in worship, and in relationships (Eph. 5:15-6:9).

c) Our walk with God is "humbly" to submit to His will because He is God and we are not.

d) In Titus 2:12 this walk with God is to live "godly." In Matthew 22:37-39 this walk is to "love the Lord your God with all your heart [with excitement)], with all your soul [your very life], and with all your mind [your thoughts are upon God]." We are to give to God what he deserves.

CONCLUSION

A. In the courtroom or God we must consider how good God is to us. Why does He not deserve the very best from us? We must see that God does not desire our service when it is just going through the motions of serving Him, but God wants our hearts. He desires that we offer our sacrifices to Him, but only when we "do justly,...love mercy," and "walk humbly with" Him.

B. If we will take this message seriously, we will know what God requires of us...and then we can set about to do it. Would you begin today?

THE CROSS OF CHRIST

(EPHESIANS 2:1-22)

JAY LOCKHART

INTRODUCTION

A. Coupled with His resurrection, the cross of Christ is the most significant event of history. The cross is the theme of Scripture, and it is the scarlet thread that runs from Genesis to Revelation.

B. Since the entire Bible is about the cross of Christ, we are not surprised that the cross is pictured in various ways in the Old Testament, including the victorious seed of the woman in the Garden of Eden, Abel's lamb, Abraham's sacrifice of Isaac, Israel's Passover lambs, the Suffering Servant of Jehovah in Isaiah 53, and the entire sacrificial system of Israel.

C. The cross of Christ is according to the eternal purpose of God (Acts 2:23), and Christ is indeed "the Lamb slain from the foundation of the world" (Rev. 13:8).

D. The cross was predicted by the Old Testament prophets, anticipated by Jesus, and preached by the apostles as the only hope for a lost world (see 1 Cor. 15:1-4).

E. Because the whole Bible presents the cross, one can preach on the cross from various passages of Scripture. This message presents the cross from Ephesians chapter 2, a passage in which we will view the cross from three directions.

BODY

A. **First, Beneath the Cross There Is Lost Humanity (1-3)** – In these verses Paul presents hard- hitting descriptive phrases which describe the Ephesians, and every accountable human being, before they came to know Christ.

   1. "Dead in trespasses and sins"

      a) They had no spiritual life because they had been separated from God by sin (Isa. 59:1-2). The basic meaning of death is "separation." When one's body and spirit are separated, we rightly say, "He is dead" (see

Jas. 2:26a). When one is separated from God, he is dead spiritually.

b) "Sins" is plural and refers to "acts of sin." The Greek word translated "sins" is *hamartia* and means "to miss the mark" (Wuest, *Wuest's Word Studies from the Greek New Testament for the English Reader; Ephesians and Colossians*, 60). It pictures an archer shooting an arrow at a target and missing, either by going beyond, falling short, or going to either side. He may say, "I have missed the mark," or, "I have sinned." This is the most common word for "sin" in the New Testament, being found about 175 times in the Greek text, showing that every time one sins, he misses the target of God's will.

c) "Trespasses" is a translation of *paraptōmasin* and means "to deviate from the right path, to turn aside" (Baker, ed., *The Complete Word Study Old Testament*, 2348). The Ephesians had missed the target of God's word and had deviated or turned aside from God's revealed will.

d) This describes every man (Rom. 3:23). The goal of everyone should be to do God's will and glorify Him. When we fall into trespasses and sins, we fail in this regard. If a person lives his entire life separated from God in sin, he will be separated from God throughout eternity (Rom. 6:23).

e) It should be noted that one may be alive physically (he goes to work, mows his lawn, watches his kids play sports), but be very much dead spiritually if he is living in sin.

2. "Walked according to the course of this world"
   a) Belonged to an alien kingdom.
   b) Literally Paul is saying the Ephesians once lived "according to the people of this age" and, therefore, did not seek to please God.

3. "According to the prince of the power of the air, the spirit who now works in the children of disobedience"
   a) Satan, who rules over the evil spiritual powers (see 6:12), dominates the lives of those who are characterized ("children") by a spirit of disobedience. Note: Greek grammar shows that "prince" (accusative

case) is not "the spirit of disobedience" (genitive case) or they would be the same case. Therefore, "the spirit" is the attitude of mind of the disobedient.

    b) Lost men belong to an alien prince, the devil.

4. "Fulfilling the desires of the flesh and of the mind"

    a) They did their own thing rather than God's thing.

    b) "Among whom" shows that they were living as the children of the world lived.

5. "Were by nature children of wrath"

    a) They were born with the nature of Adam having a tendency to sin.

    b) They were not born sinners (see Ezek. 18:20), but they were born with a human nature and were therefore sinners potentially. When they became sinners actually, that is, responsible and accountable, they were the subjects of God's wrath.

B. Second, Above the Cross There Is a God of Love (4-12).

1. "But God" – This makes all the difference.

2. While God is just and justice gives to one what is deserved (see Rom. 6:23), God wants to withhold what we deserve and show to us His mercy and His grace.

3. Justice gives to one what is deserved; mercy withholds what is deserved; and grace gives to one what he could never deserve (see verses 4-7).

4. "Grace" summarizes all that God has done to save us (8a).

5. "Faith" summarizes our response to God's grace through belief, trust, and obedience (8b).

6. "Gift" suggests we can never earn our salvation or deserve it or do enough to merit it (8c). It should be remembered that in order to benefit from a gift, one must accept it (see Tit. 2:11 and 2 Cor. 6:1).

7. "Works" (9) need to be clarified. No one can do enough good deeds (works) to put God in his debt so that He owes man salvation. Yet, faith always demonstrates itself by what it does (see the challenge of Jas. 2:17-24). Therefore, works of merit are out, but works of faith are in (see Heb. 5:9).

8. We are created in Christ as God's masterpieces ("workmanship") to continue in doing "good works." (10).

9. Until we respond to this God of grace by our willing obedience of faith, we are without hope and without God in this world (11-12). If we should die without God, we will be without God for eternity.

C. Third, Upon the Cross Is a Dying Savior (13-22).

1. "But now we who were alienated from God are able to be near to God because we are in Christ (Rom. 6:3) and because of His blood [the cross]" (13).
2. Christ is our way to "peace" with God, and the Law of Moses which separated Jew and Gentile has been "broken down" so that Jew and Gentile can be one with each other (14-15). This was a great thing that Christ accomplished, but the greatest thing He did is next.
3. Christ reconciled both Jew and Gentile to God "in one body" which is the church (16-18). There is no salvation promised to anyone who is not "in Christ" and "in one body" (see Gal.3:26-27 for the one and 1 Cor. 12:13 for the other).
4. Further, when one is reconciled to God in the one body of Christ, he is a citizen in the Kingdom of Christ (19a; see Jn. 3:5); he is a part of God's family, His household (19b; Rom. 8:17); and he is an important stone in the spiritual house where God dwells (19c-22).

CONCLUSION

A. So we see the cross. Beneath the cross we see ourselves in all of our need; above the cross we see the loving God of justice, mercy, and grace who wants us to be saved; and upon the cross the only Savior of a lost and ruined and wrecked world.
B. When lost men hear the message of the cross, the power of God to save (1 Cor. 1:18), the angels of heaven hold their breath as they watch to see who will respond to the gracious provision of God in Christ.
C. Will you respond now?

THE EXCELLENCE OF CHRIST (HEBREWS 1:1-4)

JAY LOCKHART

INTRODUCTION

A. Who is the greatest person you have ever known? Who is that one person who, in your mind, surpassed all others in greatness? Was it a parent? Was it a teacher? Who was it for you?

B. There have been many great people walk across the stage of life.
1. In the Bible we think of Noah, Abraham, Moses, and the prophets. We think of Peter, Paul, Barnabas, and others.
2. In the history of our country there are names like Washington, Jefferson, Lincoln, and too many others to mention.

C. But the one person who surpasses all others and is superior to everyone in greatness is Jesus Christ of Nazareth, the Son of God, the Savior of the world.
1. The writer of the Book of Hebrews said that Jesus "has by inheritance obtained a more excellent name than" even the angels of heaven (Heb. 1:4).
2. The English word "excellent" is a translation of the Greek word *diaphorōteron* and means to be superior, to be greater, to be surpassing, and to be different. The angels are God's "messengers," but Jesus is by inheritance the "only begotten Son of God."
3. The term "name" is that by which one is known and in respect to Christ speaks of His identity, His power, His position, and His authority—He is different from all others in that He is beyond comparison; He is surpassing, greater than, superior to, more excellent than even the angels.

BODY

A. The Excellence of Christ Identified
1. The Book of Hebrews was written to Jewish Christians who lived in the Land of Palestine. By the first century the Jews were scattered throughout the Roman world, and

those who lived outside Palestine had largely adopted the Greek language and the Greek culture and were called Hellenists or Grecians (compare Acts 6:1 in the KJV and the NKJV). The Jews who lived in Palestine spoke Aramaic (a variation of Hebrew) as their language of choice and held more to traditional Jewish ways than did the Jews who spoke Greek.

2. The Jewish Christians who lived in Palestine were under pressure from their relatives and friends, who had not accepted Christ, to give up Christianity and to return to Judaism. The temple was still in Jerusalem, Jewish worship continued, and the Christians were persecuted. Therefore, many of them were about to leave Christ and to return to Moses and the Law.

3. To prevent this apostasy the writer of Hebrews presented the excellence of Christ as he showed that Christ is superior to Moses and everything connected with the Law so that these Christian Jews would be extremely foolish to leave Christ and the gospel for Moses and the Law. In comparing and contrasting the Gospel and the Law the writer of Hebrews used the word "better" about a dozen times to describe the Gospel.

B. The Excellence of Christ Demonstrated

1. *Christ is God's Prophet* to this age (1:1-2). One of the greatest announcements of all time is made in the opening lines of Hebrews 1 when the writer said, "God,…has…spoken." The writer divided all of time into two parts: "…in time past;" and "…these last days." In former times (the Old Testament days) God spoke at various times and in various ways unto the fathers by the prophets. In these last days (since God has been speaking to us through Christ we have been in the last days as this is the last age of the world's existence) God has and is speaking unto us through His Son (see Matt. 17:5). The context of Matthew 17 shows us that to know the will of God for us today we do not go back to Moses and the Law or to Elijah and the Old Testament prophets, but we come to Christ to hear Him.

   a) The term "prophet" means simply "one who speaks for

another " (see Ex. 4:14-16; 7:1). Christ is God's prophet to this age and speaks with all the authority of God (see Matt. 28:18).

b) Christ is superior to the Old Testament prophets, and we are to teach and preach primarily the New Testament, the Gospel of Christ (Mark 16:15; 1 Pet. 4:11).

2. *Christ is heir of all things* pertaining to God (1:2). God owns everything (Ps. 24:1), and Jesus said, "All things that the Father has are Mine' (John 16:15).

3. *Christ is the agent in God's creation* (1:2). God the Father created the world (Gen. 1:1; Acts 17:24), but He did it through Christ (Jn. 1:3), who is the agent of the creation (Col. 1:16-17). Incidentally, the Holy Spirit, the third person in the Godhead, gave order to and beautified the creation (Job 26:13). All three of the members of the Godhood were involved in the creation of the world.

4. *Christ is the brightness of God's glory* (1:3). "Brightness" is a translation of *apaugasma* and means that Christ radiates the glory of God (see 2 Cor. 4:6; John 1:14, 18).

5. *Christ is the express image of the person of God* (1:3). Christ is the exact manifestation of all the qualities of God (John 14:9; Col. 1:15).

6. *Christ upholds all things by the word of His power* (1:3). Christ is the power which directs and sustains the universe.

(Illustration) The planets of our solar system (one of many solar systems in the universe) rotate upon their axes, and they never get out of their orbit or run into each other. If the earth rotated a bit slower, it would be drawn into the sun and we would all burn up. If it rotated a bit faster, it would fly off into space and we would all freeze to death. However, it rotates at just the right speed so that it might sustain life, and this happens by the power of Christ.

7. *Christ is our Priest* (1:3). As the Prophet, Christ represents God to us. As our Priest, Christ represents us to God. A priest offers sacrifice for the sins of the people. However, Christ is not only the One who presents the sacrifice to

God, but He is the sacrifice as well. The text says, "When He had by Himself purged our sins." Hebrews 9:26 says Christ "put away sin by the sacrifice of Himself" (see Heb. 7:27; 9:26; 1 Cor. 9:26). Christ purged or cleansed us from sin by the blood of the cross (Rev. 1:5).

8. *Christ is our King* (1:3). When Christ had sacrificed Himself for us, he "sat down at the right hand of the Majesty on high," where He reigns as "King of kings and Lord of lords" (1 Tim. 6:15). Because He is our King, we owe our complete and faithful allegiance to Him (Lk. 6:46).

9. *Christ is better than the angels* (1:4-14). Here the author uses no fewer than ten Old Testament quotations to prove his point. He begins (verse 5) and ends (verse 13) by raising two rhetorical questions showing that Christ is superior to angels, who had something to do with the giving of the Law (see 2:2; Gal. 3:19; Deut. 33:2). If Christ is better than angels and angels were involved in the giving of the Law, then the Gospel which Christ gave is better than the Law which angels gave.

10. *Christ is the Savior* (2:9). After the writer spoke of the creation, the purpose, and the fall of man (2:1-8), he presented Christ, the God-man, as the Savior of fallen man. In saving us Christ became one of us, died for our sins, and has been glorified (2:9). He has brought us to glory, is our "captain" (champion), and is not ashamed to call us His brothers (2:10-11). By His death Christ has destroyed the one who has the power over death, the devil (2:14).

C. The Excellence of Christ Accepted

1. It is imperative that we respond in the right way to the Christ of excellence.

2. There are three things we should consider from the Book of Hebrews as we respond to Christ.

   a) Let us *listen to Christ (2:1-3)*. "Therefore, we must [the imperative] give the more earnest heed [give careful attention] to the things we have heard (the gospel), lest we drift away [allow the current of various pressures to cause the ship of our lives to stray off the course of Truth through carelessness or neglect]" (2:1, emphasis added — JPL). Under the Law each "transgression" (a deliberate failure by commission) and "disobedience" (a refusal to hear by omission) received a just retribution (2:2). Therefore, we will not escape the penalty of violating the better covenant of the gospel which was spoken by the Lord and His disciples and was confirmed by miracles (2:2-4).

Let us hear Christ!

b) Let us *recognize that there is an urgency about hearing Christ* (3:7). We must respond to Christ at once.

c) Let us *continue to follow Christ*. Let us *grow spiritually* (6:1). Let us *worship* in assembly as we draw near to God for praise; as we remember Jesus Christ by holding fast to our confession; and as we encourage each other (10:22-25). Let us *serve God acceptably with reverence and awe* (12:28).

CONCLUSION

A. So, who is the greatest person who has ever lived? It is Jesus!

B. As we think of His excellence, let us accept Him into our lives now.

1. Let us hear Him as He speaks to those who have never known Him (Mk. 16:16). Let us hear Him as He speaks to our need for faithfulness (Heb. 3:12; 1 John 1:9).

2. Let us act at once with urgency (2 Cor. 3:1-2).

3. Let us grow as Christians; let us worship regularly; let us serve with awe.

121

I AM PRAYING FOR YOU

(COLOSSIANS 1:9-14)

JAY LOCKHART

INTRODUCTION

A. What do you suppose the Apostle Paul looked like? We neither know nor need to know, but it's an interesting question to ponder. There is an uninspired physical description of Paul that comes to us from the unknown author of a second-century work entitled *The Acts of Paul and Thecla,* which became so popular that it was translated from the original Greek into Latin, Syriac, Armenian, Slavonic, and Arabic. The description may or may not be accurate, but it says that Paul was short in stature, bowed in legs, hooked in nose, eyes close together, brows met in the middle of his forehead, and bald in head. It reminds us of how the Corinthians described Him: "...his bodily presence is weak" (2 Cor. 10:10).

B. Whatever his physical appearance might have been—here was a man. He was born in Tarsus, a leading city of Cilicia, educated in Jerusalem at the feet of the great doctor of the Law, Gamaliel, and scholastically standing head and shoulders above his contemporaries. His training and his zeal for the Law convinced him that Jesus was an impostor. Therefore, he became a persecutor of the followers of Christ and pursued Christians even to distant cities.

C. Then came the meeting with destiny. On a road leading to Damascus in Syria the Lord appeared to Saul, who became Paul, became a believer and was told to enter Damascus "and you will be told what you must do" (Acts 9:6). After three days the preacher, Ananias, found a believing, penitent Saul and told him, "Arise and be baptized, and wash away your sins" (Acts 22:16). Thus, Saul became a Christian; and, as he began immediately to preach the gospel which he had tried to destroy, the persecutor became the persecuted.

D. During the following years this little Jew would travel over 6000 miles by foot, on the back of an animal, and aboard a crude ship to carry the gospel to the Roman world. He would be stoned at Lystra, imprisoned at Philippi, scorned at Athens, mobbed at Ephesus, driven out of town at Thessalonica, arrested at Jerusalem, and imprisoned in Rome. From Rome he wrote four "Prison Letters" to his friends (Ephesians, Philippians, Colossians, and Philemon).

E. In his letter to the Colossians, he said in our text, "I am praying for you."

BODY

A. Paul Prayed (9 a)

1. Paul had not visited Colosse. Paul visited major population areas and sent others to outlying towns and villages. Epaphras (1:7; 4:12) may have been converted by Paul at Ephesus on his 2nd Missionary Journey and then sent with the gospel to plant the church in his home town.

2. While visiting Paul in Rome, Epaphras had told him about how well the church was doing in These aspects:
   a) Faith (4) – Their link with God;
   b) Love (4) – Their relationships with each other;
   c) Hope (5) – Their assurance for the future.

3. Having received word about the Colossians, Paul did not "cease to pray for" them. "Cease" is present indicative which indicates that the speaker is praying while he is making the statement (Zodhiates, 869), and "praying" is a present participle which shows continuous or repeated action whether in the past, present, or future (Zodhiates, 867), so Paul had been praying, was praying, and would continue to pray for them.

4. Paul must have had a very long prayer list in that he said in many of his letters that he was praying for his friends and, additionally, he was always specific about what he was praying.

B. Why Paul Prayed

123

1. Out of gratitude for what he had heard about them from Epaphras (3-8).
2. To prepare them for facing subtle error that Epaphras told him was threatening the church:
   a) Judaistic problems (2:11-16) – Is the gospel sufficient without binding certain portions of the Law on Gentile converts?
   b) Roots of Gnosticism (2:8-9) – Is the Christ of the gospel sufficient to reconcile man to God or must there be other intermediators?

C. What Paul Prayed (9-14)

1. "That you may be filled with the knowledge of His will" (9a).
   a) Knowledge comes from study, and study results in greater faith (Rom. 10:17). The Greek term for knowledge here is *epignosis*, which goes beyond simply "informational knowledge" (*gnosis*) and means an acting and motivational knowledge that comes from a personal relationship with God in Christ (see Wuest, 18 and Zodhiates, 378, 624). This knowledge will overcome every attack of Satan upon the church.
   b) From a study of the Word we come to know the revealed mystery of God (1:26); that Christ is indeed sufficient for our spiritual needs (1:15 ff.); that the gospel is the sufficient for salvation (2:8, 18-23); and the Word is sufficient for overcoming error and for accomplishing Christian development (3:1-4:6).
   c) Study results in growth (1 Pet. 2:2), discernment (Heb. 5:14), and the ability to teach ohers (Heb. 5:12).
2. "In all wisdom and spiritual understanding" (9 b).
   a) As we study, what do we need more as we study than an understanding of the message and the wisdom to apply it?
   b) Bible study must be undergirded with prayer for understanding and wisdom (see Jas. 1:5).

3. "That you may walk worthy of the Lord, fully pleasing Him" (10 a).

   a) "Worthy" translates *axios* and does not mean that we are worthy in ourselves to be accepted by the Lord but that we, through a knowledge of the Word and prayer, can live a life that is "suitable, proper" (Thayer, 53), in harmony with who we are in Christ.

   b) Living in this way brings the pleasure of God as we (now notice four participles) will: "bear fruit" (10), increase in "the knowledge of God" --get to know God better (10), be strengthened" by God's power (11), and be "giving thanks" for all that God is doing in our lives (11-14).

4. "For all patience and longsuffering with joy" (11).

   a) "Patience" translates *hupomone* and means "endurance as to things and circumstances" (Zodhiates, 964).

   b) "Longsuffering" translates *makrothumia* and means "enduring with people" (Zodhiates, 934). What else do we deal with? People who disappoint us and circumstances which beset us. When this prayer of Paul is answered in your life, you can find the strength to deal with every person you meet and every circumstance you encounter.

   c) "With joy" means we do not bear long with people and circumstances with resignation, but with joy.

   (Illustration) A number of years ago I visited London, England. When one goes to London, one of the things to see is Buckingham Palace, the home of the Queen.
   Our guide told us to notice that the Union Jack (England's Flag) was flying over the palace.
   He said when the Queen is at home the flag flies, but that when she is away, the flag does not fly. The flag flying tells the Brits that the Queen is among them and they can rejoice. In a similar way, when the growing Christian meets the people and circumstances of life with joy, it may be a sign that Christ is dwelling with him.

CONCLUSION

A. Paul's prayer for the Colossians is my prayer for you...and me. As we come to a deeper understanding of Scripture through study and prayer, we will lead lives that are pleasing to God; and we will bear the right kind of fruit in our lives. This will lead to a meaningful relationship with God; and, as we know God better, we will receive strength through His power to deal with people and circumstances with joy. Finally, we will be people filled with gratitude for all that God has done for us! Indeed, He has qualified us to be His heirs by placing us in the Kingdom of His beloved Son as his redeemed and forgiven people (see the text).

B. Let us be this people...and let us live before a watching world as this people.

> "I'd rather see a sermon
> Than hear one any day;
> I'd rather one should walk with me
> Than merely tell the way."
> --Edgar Guest

REFERENCES

Thayer, Joseph Henry. *Greek-English Lexicon of the New Testament*. New York: Harper, 1889; reprint Chicago: American Book, n.d.

Wuest, Kenneth S. *In These Last Days*. Wuest's Word Studies, Vol.4. Grand Rapids: Eerdmans, 1966.

Zodhiates, Spiros. *The Complete Word Study Dictionary: New Testament*. Iowa Falls: World Bible, 1992.

THE SUFFERING SERVANT OF JEHOVAH

(ISAIAH 53:1-6)

JAY LOCKHART

INTRODUCTION

A. Once two men met on a dusty road between Jerusalem and Gaza. One of the men, a man from Ethiopia, was in a chariot, on his way home following a journey to Jerusalem, where he had gone to worship. He had been reading from the scroll of Isaiah the prophet, and the place he was reading said this: Acts 8:32-33.
   1. The other man was Philip the evangelist, who had been sent to meet the Ethiopian (Acts 8:26-30).
   2. A question and the answer (Acts 8:30-31).
   3. After asking Philip to sit with him, the Ethiopian asked another question, and the evangelist preached from the passage the message of Jesus (Acts 8:31, 34-35).
   4. The result was that the Ethiopian became a Christian (Acts 8:36-40).
      Note: Preaching Jesus must of necessity include a discussion of the action and purpose of baptism or the Ethiopian would not have known to ask the question of verse 36.
B. This event emphasizes the fact that from eternity almighty God saw all of history as though it had already happened.
   1. He saw the creation and fall of man (Gen. 1:26-27; 3:1ff.).
   2. He saw a plan to rescue man from the fall by the death of Christ (Gen. 3:15).
   3. He saw fallen man redeemed, forgiven, reconciled to Himself, and added to the "called out" and saved people for His own possession, the church (Acts 2:47).
C. This plan of God, clearly seen by Him before it came to pass, was gradually made known to the sons of men.
   1. Prophets wrote about it but did not fully understand it (1

Pet. 1:10-12).

2. Angels held their breath as they longed "to look into it" (1 Pet. 1:12b).

3. Along the way God painted a portrait of the coming savior through the pen of Isaiah as the prophet wrote of the Suffering Servant of Jehovah.

BODY

A. The account begins in Isaiah 52 as God presented *the introduction of the Servant* (verses 13-15).

1. The Servant would be wise in that He would fulfill the will of God, and as a result He would be exalted (13; see Phil. 2:6-11).

2. The Servant would fulfill God's will through intense suffering — suffering that would astonish (i.e. "paralyze") those who would gaze upon His shame, sorrow, and undying love (14).

3. The Servant would "sprinkle" (startle) many as He would make atonement for sin (15; see Lev. 16:14-19 and Hebrews 10:22 for the sprinkling of blood).

4. Even kings would stand speechless as they heard about how God would save lost men through a Suffering Servant (15).

B. The account continues with the *presentation of the Suffering Servant* (53:1-9).

1. The weakness and power of God's plan (1-2).
   a) This was not man's plan (notice the question in verse 1 and 1 Cor. 2:9-10; 1:18 with "the arm of the Lord").
   b) The early years of the Servant's life (2; Isa. 11:1) — He brought hope to a seemingly hopeless situation (2a) and He was ordinary in appearance (2b).

2. He was to be looked upon as one who has no value (we did not look His way) and would be "despised and rejected" (3) — Yet He would take our pains ("sorrows") and sicknesses ("griefs") upon Himself even though we did not elevate Him in our thoughts.

3. He took our sins (our sicknesses and our pains) as His own (4a); He was struck down ("smitten") and bowed to the will of God ("afflicted") (4b); He was pierced through

("wounded") for our "transgressions" (our revolt against God) and "bruised" ("crushed") because of "our iniquities" (our wickedness) (5a); the "chastisement of our peace" (the punishment that broke down the barrier of sin between God and man were His) and "by His stripes" (blows received) "we are healed" (from the soul's disease of sin) (5b).

4. He met our greatest need as "the Lord has laid on Him" (through the violent death of the cross) all of our wicked deeds (6).
5. He voluntarily was slaughtered for us (7).
6. He was "taken from prison" (His arrest) as well as "from judgment" (His trial brought no justice as no one defended Him) and no one declared "His generation" (since He died without offspring) (8).
7. He would die among sinners, and a rich man (Joseph of Arimathea – Matt. 27:57-60) would bury Him (9).

C. The glorification of the *Suffering Servant* (53:10-12).

1. God's will was "to bruise Him" (crush) as "an offering for sin" (10a).
2. "He shall see His seed" (10b). He shall have a spiritual family (see Ps. 22:30).
3. "He shall prolong His days" (10c). He will be raised from the dead (see Ps. 22:16; Rev. 1:17-18).
4. "The pleasure of the Lord shall prosper His hand" (10d). See Eph. 1:9-10; Col. 1:19.
5. God will "be satisfied" with the Servant's sacrifice for sin and His death for the justification of sinners (11-12; see 2 Cor. 5:21).

CONCLUSION

A. Isaiah 53 is the most concise and comprehensive portrait of the Messiah to be found in the writings of the prophets.
B. It reminds us that God has been at work from eternity to bring salvation to us.
C. It should motivate us to accept the Suffering Servant of Jehovah at once in obedience to His will.

WHO DO YOU SAY THAT I AM?
(MATTHEW 16:13-26)

JAY LOCKHART

INTRODUCTION

A. In the northeastern extremity of the Land of Palestine old Mount Herman stretches more than 9000 feet toward the heavens. In ancient times there was a village near the foot of Mount Herman called Panaus, named for Pan the Greek god of nature. Long before Jesus was born in Bethlehem of Judea that little village had decayed into dust and ashes. But just before the angels said, "Glory to God in the highest, and on earth peace, goodwill toward men" in announcing the birth of Jesus, another town had been built upon that spot by Herod Phillip, who ruled that part of Palestine. He called the city Caesarea Philippi after himself and the Emperor of Rome, thus joining his name to that of the Imperial Ruler. Into the region of Caesarea Philippi Jesus came at the midpoint of his ministry with two important questions for his disciples.

B. (This introduction is a summary of the introduction that the prince of preachers in the latter part of the 19th and early part of the 20th centuries, T.B. Larimore, gave a sermon he entitled, *The Rock*).

BODY

A. The Questions Asked

1. "Who do men say that I, the Son of Man, am?" (13)

   a) Jesus had been engaged in his personal ministry for about two years, and everywhere he went he had a powerful impact upon people. Everyone, it seems, had an opinion of him, and the apostles knew those opinions.

   b) "Some say John the Baptist" (14). This is remarkable when we consider the fact that John had been murdered by Herod Antipas in Matthew 14. Yet, some must have believed Jesus was John the Baptist raised from the dead.

   c) "Some Elijah" (14). Because of the promise of Malachi 4:5, some believed that the 9th century B.C. prophet, Elijah, would appear just before the Messiah came. However, Jesus identified John the Baptist as the the Elijah who was to come. (Matt. 11:10-14). Malachi did not mean Elijah would personally appear again, but that one in the spirit and power of Elijah would come to prepare the way for the Messiah.

   d) "Others Jeremiah or one of the prophets" (14). Jeremiah was a great spokesman for God during the decline and fall of the nation of Judah.

   e) Note: all of these assessments of Jesus were great compliments to him, but Jesus was neither John, Elijah, nor Jeremiah—it's never enough to compliment Christ as the greatest man who ever lived or as the greatest teacher. We must see Him as He really is.

2. "But who do you say that I am?" (15) Of the two questions, this is the more important: did the disciples have an opinion, or did they see Him as He really is?

   a) Peter must have answered for them all when he said, "You are the Christ, the Son of the living God" (16).

   b) A blessing pronounced (17). Jesus said that Peter did not learn this answer from going to the marketplace to hear what others were saying, but from God Himself. How did God reveal to Peter and to us who Jesus is?

     (1) His perfect life (see John 19:4).

     (2) His teaching with authority (Matt. 7:29).

     (3) His miracles (John 20:30-31).

     (4) His comparison (Luke 5:8).

     (5) His acknowledgement from God (Matt. 17:5) – this came later for Peter.

     (6) His resurrection (Rom. 1:4) – this too, would be later for Peter.

B. The Promises Given

1. "I will build My church"(18)

   a) A play on words: "You are Peter" (petros), "a pebble or stone," and "upon this rock" (petra), "a ledge or a bedrock" of truth, i.e., "Upon my identity as the Son of God the church will be built"– the church is built upon the foundation, not of Peter, but of Christ Himself (1 Cor. 3:11). In Ephesians 2:20 where Paul said the church was "built on the foundation of the apostles and prophets," he meant only in the sense of their preaching about Christ.

    b) "Church" (ekklēsia) is "a called-out group of people." (See 1 Pet. 2:9-10 and 2 Thess. 2:14 for who these people are and how they were called).

    c) The "gates of Hades," the power of death itself, will not prevent this from happening.

2. "And I will give you the keys of the Kingdom of heaven" (19). The promise made here was to Peter, but in Matthew 18:18 to all of the apostles.

    a) They would activate the keys on the Pentecost of Acts 2, when the terms of entrance were announced (Acts 2:38).

    b) "Kingdom" means "the rule of God through Christ" and refers to the same people as those "called out," the church.

3. "Whatever you bind...loosed" (19). The apostles would not legislate – that is Christ's role (Matt. 28:18). A careful reading of the verb tenses used in the Greek New Testament shows that Jesus said, "Whatever you bind on earth will have been bound in heaven, and whatever you loose on earth will have been loosed in heaven."

C. The Price Paid

1. *By Jesus* (21; see Acts 20:28; Eph. 5:25).
    a) Peter misunderstood (22).
    b) Peter rebuked (23)–without Christ's death there will be no church or salvation.

2. *By disciples* (24-26)
    a) "Deny self." Say no to self in order to say yes to Christ.
    b) "Take up his cross." Crosses are for dying. We die to self-rule, to sin, to the world (see Gal. 2:20; Rom. 6:1-6, 16-17).
    c) "Follow me." Surrender, commit, and devote self.

d) One can save his life by going his own way, but he will lose real life, abundant life, eternal life. Or one can lose his life by following Christ and gaining real life.

CONCLUSION

A. Who do you say that Jesus is?
B. If you believe what Peter believed then accept His promises as true and be a part of them.
C. So, are you ready to acknowledge the price He paid for your soul and the price you must pay to follow Him?
D. The challenge to ponder – (26).

CHRIST'S DREAM FOR THE WORLD (MATTHEW 28:18-20)

JAY LOCKHART

INTRODUCTION

A. Christ has a dream for the world. The dream is revealed in what we have rightly called the Great Commission (see the text).
B. Christ's dream is to fill the world with people who are His disciples.

BODY

A. What is a disciple?

 1. A *learner* (Matt. 11:29). To learn about Christ we must know the gospel.
 2. A *follower* (Matt. 4:19). One may have knowledge of Christ but not be a disciple. A disciple puts what he has learned about Christ into practice by following Christ.
 3. An *imitator*. A disciple seeks to be like the Master (1 Pet. 2:21).
    a) The word "example" means literally "a writing pattern."
    b) When I was a child, our school rooms had the letters of the English alphabet on the wall above the black boards. I do not know why they were there except for the fact that if a child forgot how to make one of his letters, he could look above the blackboard and copy the letter he forgot. The letter above the blackboard was perfect, and the child's was imperfect, but the child's letter at least resembled the letter he copied.
    c) In a similar way the disciple looks to Christ and seeks to be like Him.

B. Why Should We Become Disciples?

 1. *To fulfill the dream of Christ.* I want to be what Christ wants me to be.
 2. Because of the *identity of Jesus*. Let us come to one of the

great discipleship passages of the New Testament to see who Jesus is: John 8:18-36.

a) Jesus claimed that God is His Father (18a).

b) Jesus claimed that He came from God (18b).

c) Jesus claimed that the Father bore witness of Him (18c). How did God bear witness of Christ?

   (1) His *perfect life*. He is one of us, yet He is above us (see Luke 5:8), and no one can ever find any fault in Him (John 19:4).

   (2) His *teaching with authority* (Matt. 7:29).

   (3) His *miracles* (Jn. 20:30-31).

   (4) The *voice of God* (Matt. 3:17; Matt. 17:5; John 12:27-29).

   (5) The *empty tomb* (Rom. 1:4).

d) Jesus claimed to be the only way to God (24).

e) Jesus claimed His cross would demonstrate who He was (28; see also 1 Cor. 15:1-4).

3. Because *I want to be free* (John 8:32).

a) What is freedom? It is not attained by doing as one pleases – this only leads to sin upon sin.

b) The freedom offered by Jesus is freedom *from* sin (8:34), *from* self-rule (see Matt. 16:24) and freedom *to* become all that Christ can make of us (see Eph. 2:10).

c) We become free by knowing that truth, the word of God (see John 17:17).

C. How Can I Become A Disciple?

1. Believe in Christ (8:30).

a) Belief that is approved by God in Scripture always involves three elements: conviction, trust, and obedience (see John 2:17).

b) Our belief is *in* Christ. It is more than believing *about* Christ or believing the *words* of Christ.

(Ill.) if a doctor tells his patient that he needs surgery, the patient may believe the words of the doctor. However, this is not belief *in* the doctor. If the patient believes the words of the doctor and says, "I want you to perform the surgery," this is belief in the doctor.

    c) When we believe *in* Christ, we are placing ourselves in His hands because we have confidence in Him.

2. Continue in His word (8:31). It is not enough to start out with Christ. We must abide or continue in His word (see the action of the verbs as a continuing process in Jn. 10:28-29 and 1 Jn. 1:7).

3. Know the truth (8:32). Know with understanding, acceptance, and obedience (Rom. 6:17-18).

    a) What is the heart of the "doctrine" preached in the first century? (see 1 Cor. 15:3-4).

    b) Paul said we obey the "form" of the doctrine. A "form" is a mold to which we conform. How do we conform to the death, burial, and resurrection of Christ? (see Rom. 6:1-6).

CONCLUSION

A. Christ wants us to become disciples.

B. We should want to be disciples.

C. We can become disciples, and it is urgent that we act at once (see 2 Cor. 6:1-2).

PART 3

EXAMPLES OF EXPOSITORY SERMONS

Sermons by Clarence DeLoach

THE TEMPLE OF THE LIVING GOD

CLARENCE DELOACH

TEXT: 2 CORINTHIANS 6:16; 1 PETER 2:4-10

INTRODUCTION

1. Before we examine the texts, let me suggest that the redeemed are pictured by several metaphors in the New Testament.
   a. A metaphor is a figure of speech in which one thing is laid over against another thing in order to make a comparison of the two. Jesus was the "master of the metaphor." (Matt 5:13; 14; John 10:9; 14; 15:1)
   b. There are metaphors that describe the redeemed.
      i. They are "children in God's family" (John 3:1-5; Gal. 3:27; Eph. 2:19).
      ii. They are "sheep in God's flock" (John 10:14; Acts 20:28).
      iii. They are "members of Christ's body" (Eph. 1:22, 23; 1 Cor. 12:27).
      iv. They are "soldiers in God's army" (2 Tim. 2:3; Eph. 6:10-18).
      v. They are "living stones in God's building" (1 Pet. 2:4, 5; Eph. 2:22).
      vi. They are "priests in God's Temple" (Rev. 1:5, 6; 1 Pet. 2:5, 9).
   c. Each one of these is vitally important to our faith. Together they present a beautiful picture gallery of what it means to be redeemed in Christ. We need to <u>drink</u> deeply from all of these images in order really to appreciate the spiritual excitement of being in Christ. They will enhance our understanding of what God is seeking to accomplish in the lives of those who know and love Him.
2. In this study, we are focusing upon Paul's affirmation, "You are the temple of the Living God," as well as Peter's extensive description of that Temple.

I. JESUS IS THE "LIVING STONE" OF THAT TEMPLE.

   A. Look at the text, "Coming to Him as to a <u>living stone</u>" (1 Pet. 2:5).

      1. How fitting that Peter, whom Jesus called Cephas (a stone), should explain to us the "Living Stone" and how we are related to Him.

      2. The emphasis in this great text is upon Jesus.

   B. Concerning Jesus, Peter says He is the Stone.

      1. That metaphor was well known to the Jewish people.

         a. Moses, in his speeches to the second generation of Israel, said, "He is the Rock, His work is perfect, for all His ways are justice, a God of truth" (Deut. 32:4).

         b. The Psalmist declared, "To you I will cry, O Lord my Rock" (Ps. 28:1), and "He only is my Rock and my salvation; He is my defense, I shall not be moved" (Ps. 62:6).

         c. And when Peter confessed his faith that Jesus was the Son of the living God, Jesus responded, "Upon this Rock I will build my church" (Matt. 16:18).

      2. That rock is the truth about Jesus! That truth is the bedrock of our faith, and it describes its stability, security, and permanence.

   C. Peter affirmed a number of the characteristics of Jesus as the Stone.

      1. He is the "<u>living stone</u>" (v.4).

         a. In Him was life (John 1:4).

         b. He came to give abundant life (John 10:10).

         c. We have been "made alive in Him" (Eph. 2:5).

         d. We have been begotten to a "living hope" by the "living word" (1 Pet. 1:22, 23).

      2. He is the "<u>chief cornerstone</u>" (vs. 6, 7).

         a. Today, cornerstones are primarily decorative, often revealing the date of the completion of the building.

         b. In biblical times, the cornerstone was the most important part of the building. A cornerstone had to be strong to support the building, and it was placed carefully since the rest of the building would be measured and kept plumb and square by it. This would be the <u>reference</u> <u>point</u> and the unifier of the whole building.

   c. Thus, it is Christ, the chief cornerstone, who unites all that God does to reconcile us together in Him (Eph. 3:3-8).

3. He is the <u>chosen</u> (elect) Stone (v. 6).

   a. He is chosen, elect, and precious! No one can take His place - not Mohammad, not Buddha, or any other religious leader. We must "hear Him!" (Matt. 17:5)

   b. He is God's anointed and chosen to be "the way" (without Him there is no going); "the truth" (without Him there is no knowing); and "the life" (without Him there is no living) (John 14:6).

4. He is the <u>precious</u> Stone (v. 6).

   a. He is honored by the Father, who twice acknowledged, "This is my Son in whom I am well-pleased" (Matt. 3:17; 17:5).

   b. As Peter had grown in Christ, he had become captivated by the word "precious" to describe Him. He spoke of –

      i. The precious blood (1 Pet. 1:19).

      ii. Precious faith (2 Pet. 1:1).

      iii. Precious promises (2 Pet. 1:4).

      iv. Precious suffering (1 Pet. 1:7).

      v. And in our text, the precious stone.

5. He is the <u>dependable</u> stone (v. 6).

   a. Those who trust Him will never be ashamed, never disappointed.

   b. Peter quotes from Isaiah 28:16, and in the Greek text, there is a double-negative used to describe those who trust Him; "they shall not, <u>no</u> <u>never</u> be ashamed."

   c. The idea here is powerful! We can totally and absolutely depend on Jesus, and our hope in Him never disappoints (Rom. 5:5).

6. But that living, chosen, precious, and dependable stone is also the <u>foundation</u> stone.

   a. No building is ever any stronger that its foundation,

and Paul affirmed, "Nevertheless the solid foundation of God stands" (2 Tim. 2:19).

 b. Jesus said, "Therefore, whoever hears these sayings of mine, and does them, I will liken him to a wise man who builds his house on the rock" (Matt. 7:24).

 c. Jesus is that "rock of ages," and what is built upon Him endures (Matt. 16:18; 2 Cor. 3:11).

7. He is also the tried stone.

 a. Isaiah's prophecy was, "Behold, I lay in Zion for a foundation stone, a tried stone" (Isa. 28:16).

 b. Here is the basis for our confidence in Him! He cannot fail because He has already been tried and tested.

 c. This gives His temple absolute assurance of His infallibility and at the same time enables us to know that He is aware and touched with the feelings of our infirmities (Heb. 4: 15).

8. That living cornerstone, chosen, precious, dependable, foundation, and tried stone is also the growing stone that Daniel pictured.

 a. Centuries before Jesus' birth, the king of Babylon had a dream in which a little stone cut out of the mountains without hands, would strike the kingdoms of this world upon their feet of clay and grow until it filled the whole world (Dan. 2).

 b. That growing stone is Jesus, and His spiritual Kingdom and that work is still in progress as the gospel of the kingdom spreads throughout the world (Matt. 28: 18-20; Col. 1:6).

9. That living stone with all of its powerful characteristics would also be the rejected stone (vs. 7, 8).

 a. He was the stone the builders rejected and the "rock of offense."

 b. He came to His own, and His own received Him not (John 1:11).

 c. Peter explained why "they stumble, being disobedient to the Word" (1 Pet. 2:8).

 d. While this statement primarily refers to the Jews'

rejection of Christ, it also speaks of all who stumble at the gospel. Paul explained, "We preach Christ crucified, unto the Jews a <u>stumbling block</u>, and unto the Gentiles <u>foolishness</u>, but unto them which are called, both Jews and Greeks, the <u>power of God</u> and the <u>wisdom of God</u>" (1 Cor. 1:23, 24).

II. JESUS IS NOT ONLY THE LIVING STONE, BUT THE BUILDER OF GOD'S TEMPLE.

A. As a young man growing up in Nazareth, Jesus learned the carpentry trade.

    1. In keeping with Jewish tradition, every boy learned a trade. When Jesus returned to His home town during His ministry, the people asked, "Is not this the carpenter?" (Mark 6:3).

    2. Jesus built things! He is the "Master Builder." He made the world (John 1:3). In Him all things consist (Col. 1:17).

    3. He built the church! He continues to expand His kingdom.

    4. He is in heaven now preparing an eternal home for the redeemed (John 14:2).

    5. Even now, in the church, we are <u>"being built</u> together for a habitation of God in the Spirit" (Eph. 2:22).

B. Through history God has dwelled with man in a number of ways.

    1. In man's earliest days, God walked with those who trusted Him (Gen. 3; 5:24).

    2. After Israel was delivered from Egyptian bondage, God instructed Moses to "build Him a sanctuary, that I may dwell among them" (Exod. 25:8).

    3. When that "tent of meeting" was completed, "then the cloud covered the tabernacle of meeting and the glory of the Lord filled the tabernacle" (Exod. 40:34).

    4. Later, when Israel was settled permanently in the land, Solomon built Him a Temple, and "the glory of the Lord filled the house of the Lord" (1 Kings 8:10).

    5. Many were the times, however, when God's covenant people misunderstood the nature of God's dwelling

among them and used the physical presence of the Temple as a false sense of security. Their reasoning was "the temple is here, the temple is here,"" though they had ceased to be God's people at heart.

6. Because of their rejection of God and His word, God removed His glory and permitted the Babylonians to destroy the Temple and the city.

C. When Jesus came in the flesh, "God dwelt [tabernacle] in the body of His own Son" (John 1:1, 14).

1. In Stephen's masterful sermon in Acts 7, he affirmed that "the Most High does not dwell in temples made with hands."

2. God dwells spiritually inside His people. God declared through His prophets, "I will dwell in them. I will be their God and they shall be my people" (2 Cor. 6:16).

3. Paul spoke of the fulfillment of that prophecy when he said, "You are God's building, do you not know that you are the temple of God and that the Spirit of God dwells in you?" (2 Cor. 3:16).

D. God places every "living stone" into His spiritual building – His Temple (1 Pet. 1:5).

1. His Temple is not completed.

2. He is still building, and God has given us the awesome privilege of being "workers together with Him" in this great venture (1 Cor. 3:9).

3. Under the Old covenant, God had a Temple for His people, but under the New covenant God has a people for His Temple. Under the Old Covenant, God's people had a priesthood, but under the New Covenant God's people **are** a priesthood (Rev. 1:5, 6).

III. CHRISTIANS ARE PRIESTS IN GOD'S TEMPLE.

A. Peter said of those "living stones" in God's spiritual building:

1. You are a holy priesthood, emphasizing the spiritual purity and sanctification of God's priests (Heb. 12:14; 1 Pet. 2:11; 2 Pet. 3:11).

2. You are a royal priesthood, emphasizing the royal robes, with which the King has clothed us.

3. He made <u>us</u> to be "a kingdom of priests" (Rev. 1:6).
   a. Under the Old system, not all of God's covenant people were priests, only those of the tribe of Levi.
   b. Under Christ, our great and better high priest, all Christians are priests, from the novice to the spiritually mature.
B. What are the implications of being God's priests, what privileges are granted, and what blessings are bestowed?
   1. Being a priest means one has access, a means of approach to the Father through our high priest – Jesus Christ (Rom. 5:2).
      a. The major point of the book of Hebrews is that "we have such a High Priest, who is seated at the right hand of the Majesty in the heavens" (Heb. 4:16).
      b. Jesus serves the "true tabernacle set up by the Lord, not men" (Heb. 9:11).
      c. He is the "mediator of a superior covenant founded on better promises" (Heb. 8:6).
      d. "He has entered the Most Holy place, once for all, by His own blood has obtained salvation for all" (Heb. 9:12).
      e. He is the long-awaited "daysman" that Job desired (Job 9).
      f. As God's priest, a Christian can offer up to God the sacrifices of praise and worship.
      g. Every Christian can confess his own sins to God and find forgiveness (1 John 1:9).
   2. As a priest of God, one has been clothed with the priestly garments.
      a. The garments of the Old Testament priests were elaborate and beautiful. They were sanctified for glory and beauty. The focus was upon physical beauty and ceremonial holiness.
      b. But the garments of God's new covenant priests are spiritual. We have put on Christ and His righteousness (Gal. 3:26, 27). His blood has cleansed and sanctified our hearts (Acts 15:9; Col. 2:11, 12). We have risen to a "newness of life"

(Rom. 6:4), and have become "new creatures" (2 Cor. 5:17). Our garments are the clothing of "tender mercies, kindness, humbleness of mind, longsuffering, bearing with one another, forgiving one another, and, above all, love which is the bond of perfection" (Col. 3: 8-13).

   c. The garments of God's priests are attractive and winsome (Acts 2:47). God's priests are "the fragrance [aroma] of Christ among those who are being saved and those who are perishing" (2 Cor. 2:15). By wearing the garments of holiness, we "<u>adorn</u> the doctrine of Christ in all things" (Tit. 2:10).

3. A priest of God, does not need to worry about daily provisions.

   a. God's Old Testament priests did not receive a land inheritance, but Levi received 48 cities with their suburbs extending out 1500 feet around them. They ate of the offerings made by fire and received the shoulders of the bulls and sheep plus the first fruits of the grain. The tithes of the people sustained them.

   b. God has promised to take care of His priests now. The same Peter who addressed Christians as a holy and royal priesthood also urged them to trust in the Lord, "casting all your burdens upon Him, for <u>He cares</u> for you" (1 Pet. 5:7).

   c. Jesus taught that to worry about food, fashion, and fitness is to live like a pagan, not as one who has a heavenly father (Matt. 6:25-34).

4. As a priest of God, one is responsible to God for his own convictions.

   a. A Christian has access to the Word of God, and he must study, do his own thinking, and equip himself to teach others (2 Tim. 2:15).

   b. What is the difference between allowing a priest, pope, or clergy to do your thinking and a brother who accepts without question what a particular school, journal, or preacher says? It was this very matter that launched the great reformation in Europe and the restoration plea in Great Britain and America.

   c. The point is — the true priest of God will study his Bible, learn what the will of God is, and form his faith and convictions accordingly.

   d. And while he respects Bible scholars, he learns never to elevate them "above that which is written" (1 Cor. 4:6).

CONCLUSION

1. Thank God! He has given us — His priests - the precious privilege of allying with Him in building His Temple (1 Cor. 3:9). We are "living stones" united and held together by the chief cornerstone. God's Temple is being built each time another stone is hewn out of sin by the glorious gospel.

2. As priests, we offer up spiritual sacrifices to God.

   a. Our bodies are offered as living sacrifices (Rom. 12:1).

   b. Our worship is offered up "a sacrifice of praise to God, that is, the fruit of our lips that give thanks to His Name" (Heb. 13:15).

   c. Our doing good and sharing is a "sacrifice well-pleasing to God" (Heb. 13:16).

   d. Winning souls is an acceptable offering to God (Rom. 15:16).

   e. Our love for one another is described as "an offering and sacrifice to God as a fragrant aroma" (Eph. 5: 1, 2).

   f. And our prayers rise up to God as "a sweet smelling incense" (Rev. 8: 3, 4).

3. Yes! You are the temple of God! You are a priest of God! You are privileged to teach the good news - to bring in the sheaves. Thus the Temple expands! Believe it! Exercise it! Live like it!

HOW DO YOU MEASURE A LIFE?

CLARENCE DELOACH

TEXT – ACTS 20:17-38

INTRODUCTION

1. The scene in this text is powerful and emotional. The Apostle Paul was revisiting several of the churches, encouraging them in the work, when he came to Miletus. Because he was in a hurry to get to Jerusalem, his plan was to bypass Asia. However, he sent to Ephesus and called the elders to meet him at Miletus.

2. It was an important meeting. They talked about their successes and difficulties. God had richly blessed the preaching of the gospel in Asia.

3. At the end of this meeting, according to verses 36-38, they held a very special prayer meeting. These men were one in the bonds of love. They had been through many prayer sessions and evangelistic meetings together; and they had shared victories and afflictions in Jesus. Now, as they meet with Paul, their spirits are melted together. They are on their knees, and tears fill their eyes.

4. As they prayed together, they realized it was their last meeting; and they began to weep. They shed not just a few tears, but they all wept freely - the King James Version says they "wept sore." Then they began to hug Paul's neck, realizing that they would see his face no more. They walked with him down to the ship, and with tears they watched him get on board. Their friend and brother was leaving, and he would be sorely missed.

5. Now, a question: "When you are gone, are you going to be missed? Will anyone, other than your family, miss you? Will your going make any difference?"
   a. Incidentally, you are going! We all are!
   b. The question is, when you go, will it make any difference?

c. How sad to come to the end of life's journey and realize that our life has been a colossal waste. Someday each of us will go out into eternity, leaving behind all that we have, and we will take with us all that we are. The question is, "What will we take with us?"

6. The world has its own yardstick by which it measures a life: intellectual brilliance, physical prowess, and monetary holdings! Brains, brawn, and bucks!

   a. The Guinness Book of World Records reveals the many unusual things that people have done to make names for themselves.

   b. But what really counts? What is important? What will last for eternity? How can we "lay up treasures" in heaven that cannot be destroyed.

   c. The text we are studying (Acts 20) reveals three important ingredients that marked Paul's life for time and eternity and determined its measurement.

DISCUSSION

I. FIRST, HIS LIFE WAS MEASURED BY THE MANNER OF IT.

   A. Look at verses 17-19: "And when they had come to him he said to them: 'You know, from the first day that I came to Asia, in what **manner** I always lived among you, **serving** the Lord with all **humility**, with many **tears** and **trials** which happened to me by plotting of the Jews."

   B. From these verses, see the manner of his life.

   1. It was a life of **humility** – "serving the Lord with all humility."

      a. There is no true greatness without humility (Mark 10:43).

      b. But what is humility? It is not putting yourself down! It is not saying you are no good! Jesus paid too great a price for you to say you are no good. If you have been redeemed by the blood of the lamb, you are a child of God! You are a "king and priest" unto God (Rev. 1:6). You are His brother, and He is not ashamed to call you such (Heb. 2:11). So don't get the idea that humility is absence of love

148

for yourself, for we are "to love our neighbor as yourself" (Mark 12:31). If we fail to regard self properly, we will not know how to love others. We are to "think soberly," i.e., appropriately of self (Rom. 12:3).

   c. So what is humility? It is not self-depreciation but it is that honest estimation of self that sees self as God sees you.

   d. The result of that proper estimation is service. "Serving the Lord with all humility" is the command. When God measures your life, He does not look to the number of servants you have, but at the number of men you serve!

   e. If your life has not been a serving life, it will amount to zero! Church members, pew warmers – listen up! You need to find your place, stir up your gift, and serve (Rom. 12:11; 1 Pet. 4:11)!

   f. If you don't serve, you won't be missed when you are gone.

2. It was a life of **heartache** – "serving with tears."

   a. Paul learned how to weep. He knew how to enter into another's pain. He was compassionate.

   b. So many live for self and self alone. They seek to insulate themselves from the toils and trials of others. They are not going to be missed!

   c. The Christian who sympathizes and empathizes – who is compassionate like Jesus - will surely be missed!

   d. Question: do the things that broke the heart of Jesus break yours? Do you ever weep? Have you wept over a soul given to addiction or one that is lost in sin? When we pray without weeping, is it any wonder that we sow without reaping (Ps. 126:5,6)?

   e. Jesus, Paul, and Jeremiah were men of tears (John 11:35, Acts 20:31, Jer. 9:1).

3. It was a life of **hardship** – "serving the Lord with trials."

   a. Paul spoke of the severe testing resulting from the plots of the Jews.

b. There were those who vehemently opposed him, sought bodily harm, and wanted him dead!

c. Paul experienced numerous "perils," but endured them all for Christ's sake (2 Cor. 11:23-28).

4. Summary – Three ingredients in Paul's manner of life: humility, heartache, and hardship. But what an impact! That is a life that will be sorely missed!

II. SECOND, HIS LIFE WAS MEASURED BY THE MESSAGE OF IT.

A. Not only are we to **live** a certain way, but we are to **speak** a certain thing. Look at verse 20: "how I kept back nothing that was helpful, but proclaimed it to you, and taught you publicly and from house to house, testifying to Jews and also to Greeks, repentance toward God and faith toward our Lord Jesus Christ."

1. Look at the **content** of his message.

a. Paul was a gospel preacher. He was convinced it was the power of God unto salvation (Rom. 1:16). It was the truth that made men free, so he kept back nothing that was profitable (John 8:32, 36).

b. There is a content of truth and we must commit to it (2 Tim. 2:2).

2. See the conviction of it (Acts 20:22-24).

a. Paul was bound by the Spirit's direction.

b. The will of God must be done, and though affliction awaited him, "none of these things move me." "I must finish my course with joy!" "I must complete my task!"

c. That is the language of conviction! A life that counts is a life with a message of right content and right conviction.

3. Observe the **confidence in** it (Acts 20:25 – 27).

a. Without a stammer he could say, "I am free from the blood of all men." What confidence!

b. Paul taught, he warned, he kept back nothing. He delivered the whole message.

c. Listen! We are "watchmen on the wall" (Ezek. 3:17-21). We must deliver God's message of judgment and warning or our own souls stand in jeopardy! Paul understood that one day he would have to report to his Lord, and he didn't want to face Him with bloody hands!

d. Think of the implications for us! We can talk easily and frequently about the weather, sports, politics, and many other subjects that in the final analysis will not amount to a hill of beans, yet we never get around to talking about what is truly important; the salvation of the soul.

e. Paul was intensely confident! Are you? Use your imagination. See Paul in that cold, dark prison in Rome. A big, burly Roman soldier knocks on his door and says, "Paul, follow me." Paul asks, "Where are we going?" The soldier says, "We are going to the chopping block, Paul, we are going to execute you. Now, put these chains on!" Paul says, "I don't need those chains, I can walk." And as they walk toward the Tiber River to the place of execution, there goes one of the greatest Christians who ever lived - hobbling along, bent and broken from the beatings, scarred from the perils and stonings. One of the guards says, "Do I hear singing?" and Paul says, "Yes, just a little song we learned promising that it will be worth it all when we see Jesus." Then the guard says, "Paul, you are strange!" When they get to the place, a soldier says, "Tie him to the block," but Paul says, "That won't be necessary." So he kneels down and puts his neck on the chopping block. "Any last words Paul?" he is asked. "Oh! Yes, I am glad you asked. Jesus Christ is Lord and Savior!" The ax falls and his head rolls over into a basket! His life here is over! Now imagine the next scene. He stands in the presence of Jesus. Paul says, "Lord, I wasn't strong! I did not have a goodly appearance! I didn't have the greatest voice! But Lord, I kept the faith, I fought a good fight, I finished my course, and these hands are free from the blood of all men."

f. Question: How would you like to meet Jesus that way? And the Lord said, "Well done, good and faithful servant, enter into the joy of your Lord." That is the measure of a great life!

III. THIRD, PAUL'S LIFE WAS MEASURED BY THE MOTTO OF IT.

A. There was something that motivated him.
   1. Note verses 33 – 35, and you will see what constrained him: "And remember the words of the Lord Jesus, that He said, 'It is more blessed to give that to receive.'"
   2. Here is the **motto** of his life: he lived his life, not primarily as a receiver, but as a giver.
   3. The result was abundant blessings. People are divided into two categories: the Takers and the Givers. The takers eat better, but the givers sleep better!
   4. It is more blessed to give than to receive. When you die, all that you will take with you is what you have given away! What you spent is gone forever; what you did not spend is left to others; but what you gave away is yours forever.

B. Please consider how Paul's motto is translated into for him.
   1. It liberated him from **covetousness** – "I coveted no man's silver or gold or apparel" (20:33).
   2. It delivered him from **idleness** – "these hands have provided for my necessities, and for those who were with me" (20:34).
   3. It freed him from **selfishness** – "by laboring like this, that you should support the weak" (20:35). Paul's life was one of giving, not taking; of helping, not hurting; of loving and lifting others.

CONCLUSION

There is not a cheap, lazy way to live a great life. It is more blessed to give than to receive! Many will not be missed when they are gone; but, on the other hand, some, like Paul, will be sorely missed.

Let Paul's life inspire us! The manner, the message, and the motto of it! Let us be reminded that when we die, we will leave all we <u>have</u> behind. But we will take all we <u>are</u> with us! What **are** you?

OUR COMMITMENT TO SOUND DOCTRINE

CLARENCE DELOACH

TEXT – 2 TIMOTHY 2:1-6

INTRODUCTION

1.   Commitment to sound teaching is a major theme in the Pastoral Epistles, 1 & 2 Timothy and Titus. Both of these letters were addressed to young evangelists, namely Timothy and Titus. The message contained in these letters would insure success in Timothy's work at Ephesus and Titus' work on the isle of Crete. It is my conviction that these inspired words from Paul will result in a fulfilled ministry today as well. Consider some of Paul's injunctions.

     a.   "Charge some that they teach no other doctrine" (1 Tim. 1:3).

     b.   "If you instruct the brethren in these things, you will be a good minister of Jesus Christ, nourished in the words of faith and of good doctrine which you have carefully followed" (1 Tim. 4:6).

     c.   "Take heed to yourself and to the doctrine. Continue in them, for in doing this you will save both yourself and those who hear you" (1 Tim. 4:16).

     d.   "Hold fast the pattern of sound words which you have heard from me, in faith and love which are in Christ Jesus" (2 Tim. 1:13).

     e.   "But as for you, speak the things which are proper for sound doctrine" (Tit. 2:1).

2.   It is evident from these passages that Paul is charging these young preachers to "commit to sound doctrine." Consider these definitions.

    a.   Commitment is to engage, pledge, entrust, or bind oneself.

    b.   Sound doctrine identifies that which is whole, complete, healthy, or wholesome.

3.   The key text that I want to examine in this study is 2 Timothy 2:2: "And the things that you have heard from me among many witnesses, commit these to faithful men who will be able to teach others also." As we examine this sobering text, please consider four relevant principles for all time.

    a.   There is a "charge to take."

    b.   There is a "context to truth."

    c.   There is a "challenge to teach."

    d.   There is a "cycle of trust."

DISCUSSION

I. THERE IS A CHARGE TO TAKE.

A. Look at verse 1: "You therefore, my son, be strong in the grace that is in Christ Jesus."

    1. When you see the word "therefore," look to see what it is there for.

    2. Paul had identified the apostolic charge in Chapter 1.

        a.   "Stir up the gift of God which is in you through the laying on of my hands" (2:6). Timothy had been given the power and equipment necessary to fulfill his ministry.

        b.   "Don't be fearful" (2:7). Timothy was to overcome the spirit of timidity, perhaps connected to his youth, by continually stirring his gift, "for God has given us the Spirit of power, love, and self-control."

        c.   "Don't be ashamed of the testimony of Christ" (2:8). Though Timothy was young and timid, the resources God had given him must be used. Suffering - and not shame - would characterize his preaching.

        d.   "Hold fast the pattern of sound words which you have heard from me, in faith and love which are in Christ Jesus" (2:13). There is a pattern of sound words, words that are healthy, wholesome, and complete. The gospel is healthy and whole. Any deviation from that message is a corruption, a perversion, and thus unsound and unwholesome.

3. Paul continues the charge in chapter 2:1: "be strong."
   a. It would require spiritual strength to "declare the whole counsel of God" (Acts 20: 20, 27).
   b. The gospel ministry is no place for timid weaklings. Be strong to "hold fast the pattern of sound words." The word **pattern** translates the Greek *hupotuposis*, which was used to depict a writer's outline or an artist's rough sketch and to set the guidelines and standard for the finished work. This word has been translated as "form," "pattern," "deposit," "outline," "standard," and "example."
   c. The idea is clear! Timothy and all who would preach the gospel must above all else keep before them the model or standard of sound teaching found in the inspired deposit located in the New Testament.
4. The situation that had developed at Ephesus required strength.
   a. Some were "profane and vain babblers" (1 Tim. 6:20).
   b. Some, possibly through gnostic influence, were involved in "contradictions of false knowledge" (1 Tim. 6:20).
   c. There were those who had "made shipwreck of the faith" (1 Tim. 1:19).
   d. Others were involved in "fables and endless genealogies" (1 Tim. 1:4).
   e. Some were "idle talkers of things they did not understand" (1 Tim. 1: 6, 7).

B. Paul's charge was not only to guard or hold the standard of sound teaching, but to do it in the right manner.
   1. Note the phrase, "in faith and love which are in Christ."
   2. These qualities will give the gospel preacher invaluable characteristics:
      a. Jesus is our example of a sincere faith and a tender compassion.
      b. Paul had instructed the Ephesian church to "speak the truth in love" (Eph. 4:15).

    c. There is never any justification for an ugly, belligerent, harsh spirit in our teaching (2 Tim. 2:24).

C. There is a "charge to take," but there is also more – much <u>more</u>. Consider the following.

II. A CONTENT OF TRUTH

A. Now look at verse 2, "And the things you have heard from me among many witnesses, commit these."

  1. What were included among the "things you have heard?"

    a. It was the "gospel which Paul preached" (Gal. 1:11).

    b. It was that which came by revelation (Gal. 1:12).

    c. It was "the faith" that Paul once tried to destroy (Gal. 1:23).

    d. It was "the faith once delivered" (Jude 3).

    e. It was "the mystery" now revealed (Eph. 3: 1-3).

    f. It was the deposit, pattern, form, standard, treasure that had been entrusted to Paul.

  2. Of that "content" of truth, we can confidently affirm that it is –

    a. Infallible in its totality (Ps. 19:7, Prov. 30:5, 6).

    b. Inerrant in all its parts (Ps. 119:128).

    c. Complete in content (2 Tim. 3:15-17).

    d. Authoritative in substance (Tit. 2:15).

    e. And effective in its results (Isa. 55:11).

B. In view of all this, it is sad –

  1. When some teach that there are no absolutes, that one cannot know truth.

  2. That some brethren even deny that there is pattern authority; that there is a deposit or standard of sure and certain truth.

  3. Some view the New Testament only as a generic "love letter" and the church as nothing more than "our fellowship."

  4. Sadly, that some of our brethren are expressing "strange sounds" in their pragmatic, post-modern approach to scripture.

C. There is a **content** of truth, and the most important yardstick by which a church is measured is not how large it is, how good the fellowship is, how good the preacher is, or even how well it is respected in the community, but how it views and handles the word of God – how it teaches and lives the truth – how it guards and proclaims the truth.

D. There is a "charge to take," a "content to truth," but there is also...

III. THE CHALLENGE TO TEACH

A. Look at verse 2 again: "And the things [the deposit, the pattern, the treasure of truth] you have heard from me among many witnesses, commit these to faithful men...."
   1. Faithful men must teach, i.e., men of faith who are loyal, trustworthy, and dependable.
   2. Evangelism is a commitment. We have been given a sacred trust as stewards, and the key qualification of a steward is faithfulness (1 Cor. 4:2).

B. Preaching the gospel is a sacred stewardship to be proclaimed faithfully.
   1. "Preach the word"; be instant in season and out (2 Tim. 4:2).
   2. Our charge is a solemn charge before God, not a board, not a church, not a human organization, but before the Lord who empowers and judges.
   3. The imperative **Preach** translates the Greek *Kerrusso*, which means "to herald publicly." The word was used of the servant of the king who was assigned the task of delivering faithfully the message of the king. It was not his prerogative to modify or amend the king's pronouncement but to guard and deliver it faithfully.
   4. We, too, like Paul, have been "approved by God to be entrusted with the gospel" (1 Thess. 2: 3-11).

C. When Paul described the nature of his ministry to the Thessalonians, he used three powerful metaphors (1 Thess. 2:4-11).
   1. It was like a **steward**, entrusted with the gospel (2:4). The key idea is faithfulness.
   2. It was like a **mother**, nurturing her children (2:7). The key idea is gentleness.

3. It was like a **father**, exhorting and challenging his sons (2:11). The key idea is encouragement.

D. What a picture of the balance that should characterize our ministry of the gospel: as stewards, faithfully proclaiming the message; as a mother, tenderly nurturing her children; and as a father, charging and encouraging his sons.

IV. THERE IS A CYCLE OF TRUST

A. Look at the verse again: "And the things that you have heard from me among many witnesses, commit these to faithful men who will be able to teach others also."

1. Look at the cycle – from Christ to Paul, from Paul to Timothy, from Timothy to faithful men, and from faithful men to others also.
2. This is "true apostolic succession." It is to be passed unchanged to subsequent generations very much like the passing of the Olympic torch.
3. The true Biblical faith is the "apostle's doctrine" given by revelation and inspiration of the Holy Spirit.

B. Here is a serious and sobering responsibility:

1. We are a part of that "cycle"; others are also.
2. Are we being faithful in our own generation? May we be faithful, not to the traditions of our fathers, but to the message of the gospel described in the New Testament!
3. Are we really teaching our children, our youth, and our people? Do we take for granted that they know and understand the truth that makes men free?
4. Just one generation that is neglected will result in a generation that has no knowledge of the restoration plea, the identity of the church, God's way of salvation, and the worship described in the New Testament. That neglected generation will result in apostasy, confusion, and anarchy (See Judg. 2).

C. The church is the "pillar and support" of the truth (1 Tim. 3:15).

1. The church does not invent truth, nor is it to alter truth, but it is to support and safeguard the truth.
2. Thus the church in every generation must solidly,

immovably, and carefully affirm, preach, and defend the truth.

3. Churches that tamper with truth, depreciate it, and abandon its authority have destroyed their only reason to exist, and they are inviting the judgment of God to "remove the candlestick."

4. So how are we to uphold it, thus being the "pillar and support" of the truth?
    a. Believe it. (2 Cor. 4:13)
    b. Memorize it. (Ps. 119:11)
    c. Meditate on it. (Josh. 1:8)
    d. Study it. (2 Tim. 2:15)
    e. Obey it. (Ps. 119:2)
    f. Defend it. (Phil. 1:7)
    g. Live it. (Tit. 2:10)
    h. Preach it. (2 Tim. 4:2)

5. As a **good soldier** (2 Tim. 2:3, 4), be willing to suffer and to concentrate with discipline and dedication; as a **competing athlete,** play by the rules (2:5), and as a **hard-working farmer** (2:6), give diligence, patiently wait, and then partake of the harvest.

CONCLUSION

This great text affirms four great principles that must remain as long as the church exists on this earth. There is a charge to take seriously, there is content to the message of truth, there is the challenge to faithfully teach it, and there is a cycle of trust.

The New Testament warns of times when men would not receive "sound teaching," but would gather to themselves teachers in accordance with their own desires – teachers who would tickle their ears (2 Tim. 4:3-4). Many are filling church buildings to get their ears tickled with the gospel of self-esteem, positive thinking, and easy believism. They come to have their egos fed and their sins approved rather than to have their thinking challenged, hearts cleansed, and souls saved. The post-modern approach deliberately rejects Biblical truth and wants a feel-good" message.

It is time for the Lord's church, the Lord's people, to saturate their hearts with the text we have explored.

A BIBLICAL DEFINITION OF A CHRISTIAN

CLARENCE DELOACH

TEXT – 1 PETER 4:16; 1: 18 – 2:12

Introduction

1. It comes as a surprise to many to learn that the word "Christian" is found only three times in the New Testament. A look at the context in which the term is used reveals that being a Christian involves:

   a. A change (Acts 11:26) "And the disciples were called Christians first in Antioch." Chapters 10 and 11 of Acts focus upon the conversion of the Gentiles. The Jews who learned about it became silent, but glorified God, saying "Then God has also granted to the Gentiles repentance to life" (Acts 11:18).

   b. A choice (Acts 26:28) Then Agrippa said to Paul, "You almost persuaded me to become a Christian." Though given the opportunity, Agrippa refused to make the choice. Paul's desire was that all who hear the gospel would choose, as he did, to become a Christian.

   c. A challenge (1 Pet. 4:16) "Yet if anyone suffers as a Christian, let him not be ashamed, but let him glorify God in this matter." Suffering saints who were reproached for the name of Christ were encouraged with the promise that "the Spirit of glory and of God rests upon you" (1 Pet. 4:14).

2. That there are both disagreement and confusion over what a Christian really is, no one can deny.

   a. To some, a Christian is defined **nationally**. If one is a citizen of America, then he feels that he is a Christian, since he has concluded that America is a Christian nation. But he is incorrect in his conclusion, because the New Testament recognizes God's nation as "His own special people" (1

Pet. 2:9).

    b.   Others define a Christian in terms of **morality**. A good moral person, who lives on a high moral plane, is a good neighbor, a pleasing personality who pays his debts and respects the rights of others. But the New Testament records examples of good people who needed Christ. Cornelius (Acts 10), Lydia (Acts 16), and the Ethiopian Eunuch (Acts 8) are just a few who could be named.

    c.   Still others think of a Christian **religiously.** Just being favorable toward Christ, believing that He is divine and having membership in some denominational church are considered evidence. One may "believe" on Him and never be a Christian (John 8:30). It is noteworthy that the majority of the cases of conversion in Acts were people already deeply religious.

    d.   The fact of the matter is that a citizen of America could be a Christian, but not all citizens are Christians. A Christian will live by the moral principles of the Word of God, but not all moral persons are Christians. A Christian will exercise the teaching of "pure and undefiled religion," but not all religious people are Christians.

3. In this study, let's by-pass our pre-conceived ideas and study Peter's inspired definition.

    a.   Since Peter addressed his initial readers as "Christians," let's look into his letter for more information.

    b.   Consider those to whom Peter wrote: "To the pilgrims of the Dispersion in Pontus, Galatia, Cappadocia, Asia, and Bithynia" (1 Pet. 1:1). The sojourners of the dispersion were Jews who had left their native land and were living on foreign land amidst strangers. They were scattered among Gentile nations.

    c.   The places Peter mentions, in particular "Cappadocia, Pontus, and Asia," were represented on the day of Pentecost when Peter and the apostles preached the first gospel sermon and about 3,000 souls "repented and were baptized for the remission of sins" and were thereupon "added to the church" (Acts 2:38, 47).

d. So these scattered Christians were among the first to hear the good news of salvation available through the crucified and risen Savior.

e. Apparently, after remaining in Jerusalem for some period of time, these "Christians" returned to their homes as "strangers and pilgrims" in hostile lands.

4. While Peter's primary emphasis was to encourage them to stand firm under "fiery trials" and to strengthen them for greater endurance (1 Pet. 5:12), he reminds them of their relationship to God, how they were redeemed and how they should live as the sanctified in Christ. In this we see an inspired definition of a Christian.

DISCUSSION

I. THEIR RELATIONSHIP TO GOD - (I Peter 1:1-5)

A. Look at verse 2, "The elect of God."
1. Christians are called and chosen (Eph. 1:4; Rom. 8:28; 2 Thess. 2:14).
2. Christians are "the election of God" (1 Thess. 1:4).
3. Sadly, the beautiful doctrine of election has been perverted by Calvinism which asserts that it is arbitrary, mysterious, and unconditional.
4. Peter explains how it works, "in sanctification of the Spirit, in obedience and the application of the blood" (v. 2).
5. Paul explained to his listeners, "from the beginning God chose you for salvation through sanctification by the spirit and belief in the truth, to which He called you by our gospel" (2 Thess. 2:13, 14).
6. There is no discrepancy between God's sovereignty and man's volition to receive the call.

B. Look at verse 3, "begotten us again."
1. Christians have been "born again of the water and of the Spirit" (John 3:3-5).
2. God is our Father and we are His children (Gal. 3:27).
3. Those Peter addressed had been "born again" by the incorruptible word (1 Pet. 1:23). This new birth had occurred on Pentecost when those who heard repented and gladly received the word (Acts 2:37-41).

163

C. Note verse 4, "Heirs of God" (Rom. 8:17).
1. Christians anticipate an inheritance, according to God's eternal purpose (Eph. 1:11).
2. That inheritance is incorruptible, not subject to the corruption of material things; it is undefiled, not subject to the defilement of sin (Rev. 21:27); it fades not away like the perishables of this world, and it is reserved. God has added the names of the redeemed to the book of life.
D. Look at verse 5, "Preserved by God."
1. Christians are kept by the same power that saved them, "Kept by the power of God through faith."
2. While God "is able to keep you from falling" (Jude 24), we must "keep ourselves in the love of God" (Jude 21).
3. It is "through faith" (Rom. 10:17).
E. Being a Christian, by Peter's definition involves a special relationship with God; elect, begotten, heirs, and preserved. But, Peter – tell us more, "How are Christians made?"

II. THEIR REDEMPTION BY CHRIST (I Peter 1:18-25)

A. What is it that **redeems**? (1:18, 19)
1. Negatively
    a. It is not **corruptible things**, i.e., no material ransom is able to set us free from sin's slavery. Things that can dissolve or decay can never pay the price for our salvation.
    b. Not even "**gold and silver**," the most lasting of material things can purchase salvation.
2. Positively
    a. "But with the **precious blood** of Christ as of a lamb without blemish and without spot" (1:19).
    b. Redemption is man's greatest need (Rom. 3:22, 23). It translates the Greek *apolutrosis* and expresses the gracious work of Christ on our behalf. It expresses, along with other words like "propitiation," "ransom," "justification," "adoption" and "reconciliation," the riches of our salvation. It means "to deliver by the payment of a ransom" and

is expressed in our English word "emancipation."

    c. Redemption in the forgiveness of our sins (Eph. 1:7, Col. 1:14).

    d. No Christian has ever been made apart from "the blood of His cross" (Col. 1:20).

B. But **how** were the Christians redeemed?

    1. Look at verses 21 – 25.

       a. They believed! Verse 21 speaks of "faith" (the noun), and "believe" (the verb).

       b. On the day of Pentecost, they heard the gospel (Acts 2), and faith comes by hearing (Rom. 10:17).

    2. They obeyed the truth (1:22).

       a. They were sanctified in obedience to the message they heard (John 17:17).

       b. Christ is "the author of salvation to all who obey Him" (Heb. 5:9).

       c. Their souls were "purified in obeying the truth" (Acts 15:8, 9).

    3. Thus, they were **born again** by the incorruptible seed, the word of God (1:23).

       a. Here is a divine commentary on Jesus' words: "Except one is born of the water and the Spirit, he cannot enter the Kingdom of God" (John 3:5).

       b. A birth requires a **begettal** (1 Cor. 4:15, Jas. 1:18).

       c. A birth necessitates a **delivery** (Rom. 6:3, 4, 16-18).

C. Peter's explanation in this text parallels exactly what happened on Pentecost.

    1. The word (gospel) was preached to them (Acts 2:22-37).

    2. They heard the cutting message (Acts 2:37).

    3. They believed it, indicated by their question, "What shall we do?"

    4. They obeyed the instructions given (Acts 2:38-41).

    5. This is **how** the Christians that Peter addressed were made, and no one ever became a Christian any other way. The seed sown today will produce Christians of like kind.

III. THEIR RESPONSIBILITIES - (1 Peter 2: 1-11)

A. Redemption occurs once, but sanctification is an ongoing process which entails all that God does to mature us and make us complete.
  1. "If then you were raised with Christ, **seek** those things which are above" (Col. 3:1).
  2. The idea is "keep on seeking!" While our new life is real and powerful, so is sin. And sin can overpower us if we are not continually presenting ourselves as servants of righteousness.
B. Peter reminds those new Christians to keep on maturing in Christ.
  1. Lay aside the sins of the flesh (2:1).
  2. Desire the spiritual nourishment (2:2).
  3. Offer up spiritual worship (2:5).
  4. Exercise your holy priesthood (2:5).
  5. Live like God's special people (2:9).
  6. Proclaim the gospel (2:9).
  7. Abstain from fleshly lusts (2:11).

CONCLUSION

Peter's explanation of who a Christian is can be understood. It can be understood because God's way of salvation is simple (Ps. 119:130, Isa. 35:8). It is totally consistent with every case of conversion in the book of Acts. It is salvation by "grace through faith" (Eph. 2:8). Believe and obey today!

WHEN WORSHIP BECOMES A BURDEN

CLARENCE DELOACH

TEXT – MALACHI 1:6-14 "AND YOU SAY, WHAT A BURDEN!" (1:13)

INTRODUCTION

A. The times.
   1. Malachi, a prophet of God in the days of Nehemiah, directed his messages of judgment to God's covenant people who were plagued with corrupt priests and a false sense of security in their privileged relationship with God. Their religion had become form without function.
   2. Using the question and answer format, this messenger of Jehovah probed deeply into their problems of hypocrisy, infidelity, mixed marriages, divorce, and arrogance.
   3. Malachi has the distinction of being the last writing prophet of the Old Testament. While he is often described as a "minor" prophet, his message is "mighty." And it has a powerful relevance for our time.
   4. Ours is a time when religion has lost touch with life and worship is often a cold exercise in formalism. Our culture has become skeptical, pragmatic, and disillusioned. Ours is a time when marriage according to God's agenda is being mocked and lifestyles have become sordid and corrupt.
   5. The people were blaming God for their problems. Their words were harsh against Him, and they were saying that worship and service to Him was an exercise in futility (3: 13-15).
   6. In the text we are examining, they were saying, "Oh, what a weariness," i.e., "what a burden it is to worship God!" All the sacrifices, temple going, offerings – their worship had become tasteless and tedious! They sniffed and sneered at it – they were sick and tired of it.

B. The title, "When Worship Becomes a Burden."
   1. Can it happen to God's people today? I am convinced it has already happened to many.
   2. There are many things practiced in the religious world under the guise of worship, but much of it is self-centered and performance-oriented. Our need is God-honoring and Biblical-oriented worship.
   3. Sadly, many of God's people trudge to church week after week as though they are doing God a favor. They sit listlessly, check the bulletin, look around to scrutinize the latest fashions, and amuse themselves, but they can hardly wait until the last "amen." When it is over, they think, "Well, I have done my duty again, but what a weariness it has been!"
   4. What is the problem? Very much as with the people of Judah in our text — worship has become a painful burden to be borne. The joy, excitement, and anticipation have gone! Worship has become a chore to be endured! The fact is, many in the church have become bored with serving God, and worship has become dry and unexciting.

C. The text - Malachi 1: 6-14
   1. As we explore the text, three powerful principles emerge that God, through His prophet-preacher, Malachi, used to remind and refresh a people whose worship had become a burden.
   2. It is one thing to become tired in the work, but something else to be tired of the work. The work of God often becomes exhausting — emotionally and physically - but as we all move closer to eternity, serving God should become sweeter with every passing day.
   3. Please drink deeply of these three reminders and become spiritually refreshed.

DISCUSSION

I. WORSHIP BECOMES A BURDEN WHEN WE FAIL TO UNDERSTAND THE *NATURE OF GOD!*

A. Look at verse 6, "A son honors his father and a servant his master. If I then am a Father, where is my honor? And if I am a Master, where is My reverence? Says the Lord of hosts to you priests who despise My name."

1. God says, "I am a **Father**, and a **Master**."
2. His is the nature of a Father
   a. We are children, sons, and we owe Him **honor**.
   b. The Hebrew word translated "honor" literally means "to attach weight to something – to take seriously."
   c. The priests were defiling His name, and the people weren't taking God seriously.
   d. The fact is – when you fail to honor god, worship will always be a bother, rather than a blessing!
   e. God would prefer that you not take Him at all unless you take Him seriously. In our Lord's letter to the church at Laodicea, He said, "I know your works, that you are neither cold nor hot. I could wish that you were cold or hot" (Rev. 3:15). Lukewarmness makes the Lord sick; it is the worst form of blasphemy. Half-hearted worship is an insult to the goodness of God! It says, "I believe You are there, but You don't inspire me – You are not worthy of my whole-hearted worship."
   f. So the first thing we need to understand when we come before God in worship is – Dear God, You are my Father, and I humbly bow in Your presence. In all I do, I honor You and Your word – the way I talk, the way I dress, the way I sing, the way I listen and participate – Oh! God, You are my Father and I honor You!

B. Then God says, "I am a Master, where is my fear?" (2:6).
   1. We owe God respect, reverence, fear!
   2. What kind of fear is this? It is a godly, healthy, righteous reverence. It does not mean that we quake in our boots when we think of God. Because of the work of Christ on our behalf, we are urged to "come boldly to the throne of grace, that we may obtain mercy and find grace to help in time of need" (Heb. 4:16).
   3. A Christian is a bond-servant, that is, one whose will has been yielded to Christ because of being purchased out of the market place of sin and consecrated to His service. We have been redeemed, thus "bought with a

price" to glorify God in our spirit and in our body (Rom. 6:17, 18; 1 Cor. 6:20).

4. Thus, two things that will remove the burden from worship are namely, God is your Father and God is your Master!

   a. It is sad when brethren sit listlessly in the assembly (Ps. 89:7).

   b. Fear is love on its knees, and those who honor and fear Him love Him best (Eccles. 12:13).

II. WORSHIP BECOMES A BURDEN WHEN WE FAIL TO REVERENCE THE *NAME OF GOD!*

A. Note verse 6 again: "It is you, O priests, who show contempt for My name."

   1. The old covenant priests, from the tribe of Levi, were those designated by the law as teachers of the law and official administrants of the sacrifices required of the people. They had the audacity to ask, "How have we shown contempt for Your name?"

   2. Before we get to God's answer, let's fast forward to the New Testament and ask, "Who are God's priests today?"

      a. Every redeemed soul is a priest.

      b. John wrote, "...He has made us kings and priests to His God and Father" (Rev. 1:6).

      c. Peter described those who were "born of the incorruptible seed, the Word of God," as part of a "holy" priesthood and a "royal" priesthood (1 Pet. 1:23, 2:5, 9).

B. How did those priests in Malachi's time show contempt for God's name?

   1. They did it with their "offerings and sacrifices" (2:7, 8).

   2. They made the "table of the Lord" contemptible by offering polluted, defiled bread on the altar.

   3. They offered blind, crippled, and diseased animals to God. God said, "This is wrong, try it on your governor and see if he is pleased!"

      a. God had stipulated to His covenant people that every offering made to the Lord was to be without blemish, a male of the first year (Exod. 12:3-6).

     b. Two important principles emerge: 1) God has always required the best, and 2) Those sacrifices pictured the perfect Son of God, the "lamb without spot or blemish" (1 Pet. 1:19).

     c. By offering lame, blind, and crippled animals, they were not only insulting God, but they were showing contempt for the holy "Son of God" whom He would send to redeem sinful man.

4. The relevant lesson is evident. Do you want your worship to come alive with joy and blessing? To rise above burden to blessing? Then give to God your best!

     a. The principle is — "Where your treasure is, there your heart will be" (Matt. 6:21).

     b. It is a fact that many have an empty, heartless worship because they have never given anything significant to God. They give Him the cast offs, throwaways, and hand-me-downs.

     c. The Macedonian Christians, though in deep poverty, experienced an "abundance of joy" and "riches of liberality" because "they first gave themselves to the Lord" (2 Cor. 8:1-5).

C. We treat human beings better than God, and then we wonder why we don't get more from worship.

1. God challenged the people, "Try offering them to your governor! Would he be pleased?" (2:8).

     a. The point is, we pay our taxes! We try to fulfill our obligations as citizens!

     b. When April 15th comes, can you imagine sending leftovers and excuses? Will Uncle Sam be pleased?

     c. Yet, we often eat the cake and give God the crumbs.

2. An illustration of giving God our best. (2 Sam. 24: 10-25)

     a. David had sinned in pride and foolishness in numbering Israel. As a consequence of God's judgment, God offered David three choices. David chose three days of plague upon the people.

     b. David wanted the plague stopped because seventy thousand died. God's prophet, Gad, told him to build an altar to the Lord.

    c. Araunah owned a threshing floor, and David wanted to buy it, but it was offered free of charge along with oxen, wood, and implements for sacrifice.

    d. David's reply was classic: "No, but I will surely buy it from you for a price, nor will I offer burnt offerings to the Lord my God with that which costs me nothing" (2 Sam. 24:24).

  3. The priests and people of Malachi's time had forgotten this principle. And many of God's people today have failed to realize that worship that does not cost us something can mean very little to God.

III. WORSHIP BECOMES A BURDEN WHEN WE FAIL TO RECOGNIZE THE *NOBILITY OF GOD*

A. Look at verse 14, "For I am a great King, says the Lord of Hosts."

  1. He is King, great in power, authority, and majesty.

  2. We have seen three things about God that should inspire true worship from all who are in covenant with Him.

    a. He is our Father to be honored.

    b. He is our Master to be reverenced.

    c. He is our King to be served.

B. "Bring forth the royal diadem and crown Him Lord of all."

  1. He is a Father who can hear me and a King who can answer me.

  2. The sympathy of a Father and the sovereignty of a King – all wrapped up in our awesome God (Ps. 23:1, Neh. 4:14).

C. Listen! In true worship we are in the highest company we will ever know.

  1. Our God is "high and lifted up" (Isa. 6:1, 2).

  2. Jesus, our loving Savior and Intercessor, is present when we worship (Acts 2:36, Philem. 2:9).

CONCLUSION

  1. Has worship become a bore, a burden, a cause of weariness? Then, please remember that God is your Father; as a son,

honor Him! He is your Master, serve Him! He is your King, be subject to Him!

2. Remember His nature, His name, and His nobility. Three things that will put the zest, the thrill, and the life back into your worship and service to God!

3. As sons, give Him your honor! As servants, give Him your labor! As subjects, give Him your loyalty! Worship, then, will become an anticipated, joyful, and fulfilling experience.

WORTHLESS VS. ACCEPTABLE RELIGION

CLARENCE DELOACH

TEXT – JAMES 1:26-27

INTRODUCTION

1. The book of James is an inspired treatise on the practical side of Christianity. It is to the New Testament what Proverbs is to the Old Testament. It emphasizes the behavior of belief. True religion is more than believing the right things; it is behaving in the right way. However, behaving the right way grows out of believing the right things. If Christ has been impressed upon our hearts, He will be expressed in our lives. Simply stated, the theme of this short book of 5 chapters is, "Christianity in shoe leather."

2. Our text, James 1: 26, 27, contrasts two kinds of religion – vain and pure, supernatural and superficial, worthless and acceptable.

   a. The fact is we are drowning in religion. There are several world religions. They come in all stripes and varieties. It appears that nearly everybody has a kind of religion. And those who disdain any semblance of organized religion have in many cases their own. Most of the religions of modern culture are subjective, self-centered, and man-made. They are vain, empty and this world centered. They provide no meaning to life and have little impact upon moral and spiritual values.

   b. We are living in serious and challenging times. Are we on the threshold of world disaster? Will our country disintegrate? Or will there be a national revival? We do not know what the future holds, but we know **who** holds the future! And while we may not know the answers to many troubling questions, one thing is sure: God's people – Christians, those who have confessed Jesus and seek to serve Him, i.e. the Church - ought to be living in keeping with the urgency of these times. We need in our faith a vibrant reality, a real religion.

c. Our text naturally divides itself into two major parts.

DISCUSSION

I. THE DECEPTION OF SUPERFICIAL RELIGION

A. Note vs. 26, "If anyone among you thinks he is religious, and does not bridle his tongue but deceives his own heart, this one's religion is useless."

1. The word James used for "religious" *threskos,* is a word used for ritual, routines, and ceremony. It could be used to denote external forms. There is another word used for worship that pleases and honors God, and that is *eusebeia,* which means godliness and holiness.

2. The point is that one might think he is right in outward form, but be deceived if his conduct is not right.

B. In this verse James identifies three dangers.

1. The first is it lacks **reality.**

   a. Some may **seem** to be religious; they think they are.

   b. They have a "form of godliness" but have denied the power thereof.

   c. They have a name that they are alive, but are dead (Rev. 3:1).

   d. Religion can be an illusion – a religion without reality. It is a farce and not a force!

   e. Fellow Christian! Your religion ought to be real, sincere, vibrant – not a maybe-so, but a know-so salvation. The fact is that many professed believers are question marks when they ought to be exclamation points! Too many are seeming Christians when they ought to be sincere Christians! We need a calm confidence, a vibrant reality.

   f. Let Paul's confidence be a tonic for your spirit: "for I know whom I have believed and am persuaded that He is able to keep what I have committed to Him until that Day" (2 Tim. 1:12).

   g. Here is a confidence builder – take your Bible and read I John and circle every "know" you find. Our

175

second birth ought to be just as real as our first. There must be reality – an assurance of our salvation. Superficial religion lacks reality.

2. The second danger is it lacks **restraint**.
   a. "If one seems to be religious, but bridles not his tongue, this man's religion is vain."
   b. Practically, James is saying that one's religion will be evident by the way he talks. In fact, James gave an entire chapter to the proper use of the tongue (Ch. 3). In James 1:18, 19, he talks about the new birth (1:19), and the new behavior that follows, i.e., "swift to hear, slow to speak, and slow to wrath."
   c. The old life is one of criticizing, carping, and cursing, while the new life is one of praise and prayer. James uses the tongue to illustrate the fact that when one is saved, his life is changed, and if his religion has not changed him, then he needs to change his religion.

3. Thirdly, superficial religion lacks **results.**
   a. "His religion is vain", i.e., unproductive, fruitless, worthless – an exercise in futility, a colossal waste of time.
   b. Many think there is great value in religion, yet many are religious, but lost! Most of the conversions recorded in the book of Acts were people who were already religious, but their religion was vain, empty, and meaningless.
   c. Christianity is not just one more religion! It is not an appendage added on! It is not a code or a creed! It is "Christ in you, the hope of glory" (Col. 1:27). It is a living, growing relationship with our Lord. Without that relationship, it is a futile exercise in illusion. It is Christ inside us that changes us on the outside.
   d. We can be lost with baptismal certificates, offering records and good attendance if Jesus Christ is not real in our hearts and lives.

II. THE DELIGHTS OF PURE RELIGION

A. Note verse 27: "Pure and undefiled religion before God and the Father is this; to visit orphans and widows in their trouble, and to keep oneself unspotted from the world."

   1. In contrast to worthless, vain, futile religion, this is the religion that God accepts.

   2. James is not speaking of what may seem best to us, best to other believers, or what is best to the world, but genuine religion that meets God's standard.

B. James describes real religion in three dimensions.

   1. First, it reaches upward.

      a. "Before God, our Father."

      b. It begins by knowing God as our Father, and the only way to know God as our Father is to know His son as our Savior (John 14:6).

      c. The idea of the universal Fatherhood of God and the universal brotherhood of man is false. The Bible does not teach this; in fact, Jesus once said to the arrogant Pharisees, "You are of your father, the Devil" (John 8:4). God is the Father of those who have been "born again," i.e., penitent, obedient believers (Jas. 1; 18). Those who hear, believe, and obey the word of truth are begotten of the Father and become His children.

      d. True religion begins with God and reaches up to the Father. You cannot pull yourself up to God by your own bootstraps. You cannot work yourself up to God anymore than a man can work himself out of quicksand. Sin is like quicksand – the more you panic and struggle, the deeper you plunge. The song has it right: "From sinking sand He lifted me, with his own hand He lifted me." The Psalmist expressed it, "He also brought me up out of a horrible pit, out of the miry clay, and set my feet upon a rock, and established my steps" (Ps. 40:2).

      e. True religion is reaching up and placing a hand of faith into His hand of grace. "For by grace are you saved through faith" (Eph. 2:8).

   2. Second, pure religion reaches **outward**.

a. Pure religion is "to visit orphans and widows in their trouble."

b. Having received His grace and compassion, we will be gracious and compassionate toward those in need.

c. The word translated visit, *episkeptomia*, means much more than a social visit; it expresses the idea of caring for and helping in any way needed, even strengthening and encouraging.

d. The "orphans and widows" were about the neediest people when James wrote. There were no welfare programs, insurance or social security. Without parents or husbands, a person would be in a desperate situation. True compassion would reach out to any needy one. No doubt, James used "orphans and widows" to represent all who are in distress.

e. Our world is filled with needs and hurts of all kinds, and our Lord ministers to them through us (Matt. 25:35-36). You have been saved to serve! And when you reach out to help someone in distress, you demonstrate the transformation that has occurred in your life.

f. Someone needs your love, and Jesus has no hands but yours. He has no feet but your feet, no tongue but yours – no eyes, no ears but yours. His plan is to work through you, and if your religion is real, you will not only show up on Sunday, but on Monday through Saturday to serve in a practical way. The marvel of true religion is God working through ordinary people to accomplish extraordinary things.

3. Third, acceptable religion reaches <u>inward</u>.

a. See verse 27: "...and to keep oneself unspotted from the world."

b. The verb *tereo*, translated "to keep," indicates a continuous, perpetual conduct that is unstained by the world. The renewing of the mind means that we will not conform, but be transformed (Rom. 12:2).

   c. What does James mean by "the world"? He is not talking about the physical planet, or the world of nature, not even the people of the world. The word is *kosmos*, i.e., the order, arrangement, that ungodly value system called the world (see 1 John 2:14,15; Jas. 4:14; Rom. 12:2).

   d. Godly religion is a matter of holy obedience to the Word of God reflected by honesty in regard to self, selflessness in regard to others, and an uncompromising moral and spiritual stand in regard to the world.

   e. Sadly, many view Christianity as something added on. They exist as baptized pagans living a double life, going through forms on Sunday, but back to the world system on Monday with no significant transformation in their lives.

   f. Remember that true religion begins at a different source, continues on a different course, and consummates with a different conclusion.

CONCLUSION

1. May God help us to quit enduring religion and start enjoying salvation and delighting in the reality of pure and undefiled religion.

2. Here is what true religion will do for you:
   a. In the hour of sorrow, it will comfort you with a glow of confidence, expectation, and hope (Heb. 6:10; Rom. 5:1-5).
   b. In the hour of death, it will sustain and support you (2 Cor. 4:16-18).
   c. In the hour of judgment, it assures "there is now no condemnation to those who are in Christ (Rom. 8:1).

3. Is your religion superficial or real?

79873449R00105

Made in the USA
Lexington, KY
27 January 2018